Victor A. Salamone
June 27, 1976

Borgia

E. R. CHAMBERLIN

(Mansell Collection)

Cesare
Borgia
by E. R. Chamberlin

INTERNATIONAL
PROFILES

Cesare Borgia
© E. R. Chamberlin, 1969

Library of Congress Catalog Number 73–97964

INTERNATIONAL PROFILES

General Editor: EDWARD STORER

English language editions published by:

International Textbook Company Limited
158 Buckingham Palace Road, London, S.W.1

A. S. Barnes & Co. Inc., Cranbury, New Jersey 08512,
for sale in UNITED STATES OF AMERICA

Series Design: Melvyn Gill   *Pictorial Research:* F. G. Thomas
Colour Plates: Photoprint Plates Limited, Wickford, Essex
Covers: George Over Limited, London and Rugby
Paper: Frank Grunfeld (Sales) Limited, London
Text and Binding: Butler and Tanner Limited, London and Frome

1. The Papal Monarch

ALEXANDER VI· PONT· CCXVIII·
ANNO DOMINI MCCCCXCII.

Rodrigo Borgia (Pope Alexander VI) (Mansell Collection)

On 6 August 1492, the twenty-three members of the College of Cardinals who were present in Rome met in Conclave to elect a successor to the late Pope Innocent VIII. Five days later, during the small hours of 11 August, fifteen of them accorded their votes to Cardinal Rodrigo Borgia, giving him the necessary majority. He took the style of Alexander VI and was so presented to the crowd in the piazza outside. The great bell of the Capitol sounded its traditional welcome and, also according to tradition, the mob raced off to sack the palace of the successful cardinal and so mark the beginning of a new pontificate. They found little to pillage for, so certain had Cardinal Borgia been of the result of the Conclave, he had prudently removed his valuables before being immured with his colleagues.

It had been a short and relatively peaceful Conclave, for the only real issue had been a financial one. Which, of twenty-three very wealthy men, could outbid the others. To the world outside, the election of Cardinal Borgia came as something of a surprise, for he

1

was a Spaniard and the Spaniards were detested in Rome. But even before the Conclave opened, the better informed in Rome included his name on that very short list of cardinals who were *papabilè*, for he was accounted rich even in that assembly of wealthy men.

> His revenues from his papal offices, his abbeys in Italy and Spain and his three bishoprics are vast. His office of Vice-Chancellor alone yields him 8,000 gold ducats annually. His plate, his pearls, his stuffs embroidered with silk and gold, his books are all of such quality as would befit a king or a pope. Altogether it is believed that he possesses more gold and riches of every sort than all the other cardinals put together.

It was this wealth, partly inherited but mostly amassed from the revenues of the Church, that enabled Borgia to succeed in the auction of votes. The price of each vote was shrewdly related to the influence of the seller—each man who accepted a bribe was, in effect, being compensated according to the likelihood of his succeeding in a free election. Thus the ninety-six-year-old Cardinal of Venice received a mere 5,000 ducats while, at the other extreme, Cardinal Ascanio Sforza—a member of the powerful ruling family of Milan—received not only a great weight in bullion but was also promised the pick of the offices that Borgia now possessed, including the immensely lucrative office of Vice-Chancellor. The remarkably simony of the Conclave, unprecedented in degree if not in occurrence, gave substance to the epigram coined at the height of Borgia's career as pope: 'Alexander sells the Keys, the Altar, Christ Himself—he has a right to, for he bought them.'

The new pope was a stout, jovial man in his sixty-second year. 'He is tall, in complexion neither fair nor dark. His eyes are black, his mouth somewhat full, his health is splendid and he has a marvellous power of enduring fatigue. He is singularly elegant in speech and is gifted with an innate good breeding which never forsakes him.' Despite the fact that he was a Spaniard, Cardinal Borgia had enjoyed considerable personal popularity with the Roman mob, buying its shaky loyalty with splendid public festivals staged regardless of cost. The papal Curia as a whole regarded him as a highly competent diplomat, one of the few high churchmen capable of maintaining papal power in a fragmenting and increasingly hostile society.

Neither the Roman people, nor the papal diplomats, nor the European powers who welcomed, genuinely if fulsomely, the advent of Alexander VI, were particularly disturbed by the fact that he was the father of at least three families, all of whom would be maintained at the expense of the Church. It was the logical development of a centuries-old trend. It had long been the practice for every mobile relative of a new pope to hasten to Rome, on news of the election, in the confident expectation that the family's fortune was made. '*Nipoti*' was the term coined for these blood allies of a new pope who would be his allies in his battle to establish himself among powerful and jealous social equals. The pope, as spiritual head of Western Christendom, might be in a unique and unassailable position. But he was also prince of one of the wealthiest of Italian states and, as such, had to be prepared to hold his own against other princes. A blood relation was marginally more loyal than a purely political ally, if for no better reason than that each 'nephew' was aware that his good fortune was intimately linked with that of his great relative.

'Nephews' was a conveniently elastic term, embracing the closest as well as the most distant of a pope's relatives. It was Borgia's immediate predecessor, the old Innocent VIII, who destroyed the polite fiction insofar as it related to the closer relatives. 'He was the first of the popes openly to acknowledge his illegitimate children and, setting aside all established usage, to load them with riches,' a contemporary recorded. Hitherto, papal 'nephews' had usually been granted positions of power and responsibility, and made some return to the system in the exercise of their administrative talents. Italians accepted the situation with equanimity. Someone had to fill the posts and they might as well be blood relatives of the pope as strangers—and, in any case, the offices would inevitably be re-distributed on the death of the pope.

The son of Innocent VIII, however, became a simple parasite on the court itself, occupying precisely the position that the dissolute son of a lay monarch might occupy in his father's court. Moralists might protest, but practical politicians accepted the situation: Innocent was able to marry off his daughter into the royal family of Naples and his son into the scarcely less regal house of the Medici, both families gladly accepting a pope's bastard for the sake of the immense political influence thereby gained.

Initially, Borgia owed his own advancement to the beneficial practices of nepotism. He had been summoned from Spain, as a young man of twenty-five, when his uncle became pope and almost automatically created him cardinal. Thereafter, the younger Borgia moved steadily upward, as much through his own undoubted talents as through his powerful protector.

In 1460, about five years after he first came to Rome, Borgia took a certain Vanozza dei Cataneis as mistress. She belonged to the lesser nobility of Rome, and seems to have possessed few of the qualities which might have been expected to attract a brilliant and handsome young churchman clearly marked out for an outstanding career. Her family had no social or political influence, she herself was neither particularly attractive nor witty—and yet for nearly twenty-six years she remained his partner and even after she was supplanted by the beautiful Giulia Farnese, still exerted at least domestic influence upon him. It may, perhaps, have been her very sobriety, her comparative lack of lustre, that attracted Borgia. A mistress who demanded nothing, from a lover who could give her almost anything, was a rarity in Rome, and her total fidelity to him must have stood in emphatic contrast to the habits of the conventional courtesan.

In return for that undemanding fidelity Vanozza received what was evidently, to her, a gift more valuable than gold—the assurance that it would be her children who would benefit from their illustrious parentage and not those of her lover's other mistresses. Borgia had three other acknowledged children living when his association with Vanozza began, and for the eldest of these children he obtained the Dukedom of Gandia in Spain. But when the young man died, the title was transferred to Juan, his eldest son by Vanozza, and thereafter it was around Vanozza's four children—Juan, Cesare, Lucrezia and Joffre—that his dynastic ambitions were moulded.

Of all his children, Alexander loved his daughter Lucrezia the best. Even after she had become a married woman, theoretically accountable to another man, he could still reproach her bitterly for absenting herself from him. He proclaimed her accomplishments with doting joy and the grossest flattery of her was, in his ears, the mildest of praise. But she was merely a woman. Alexander could, and did, load her with unprecedented powers and honours but he was aware that the dynasty which he passionately desired to found must be ultimately established on a man. And it was Juan, not Cesare, that he chose for the great work.

In the first months of his pontificate, when his children began to emerge from their comparative obscurity now that their high destiny was apparent, it was observed that he treated Cesare with a coldness that amounted to indifference. Later, his attitude was to give rise to the rumours that Cesare was no child of his but the offspring of his great enemy, Cardinal Giuliano della Rovere, whom he had cheated of both the papal crown and a mistress. For Vanozza, it was said, had been the mistress of della Rovere before she became the virtual wife of Borgia—and certainly there was a bitter edge to

della Rovere's hostility to give substance to the tale. But though Alexander never specifically referred to Cesare ?s his son, as he referred to both Juan and Joffre, neither did he ever deny paternity. There was no love between them—that, perhaps, was unusual enough among the Borgia with their powerful family feeling for each other— but Alexander's coldness probably sprang from no other source than a dislike of having his plans for his family questioned by that family. Juan was to found the dynasty: Cesare was to maintain the family's hold on the Papacy. And Cesare objected to his role.

Cesare Borgia was seventeen years old when his father was elected pope—a year younger than Juan and five years older than Lucrezia. Long before he had been capable of making any decision for himself his career in the Church had been planned for him. He was only six years old when the reigning pope had obligingly dispensed him from the need to prove legitimacy—normally the inescapable qualification for church preferment. By the time he was fifteen he had already collected sufficient benefices to make him a very wealthy young man—Protonotary of the Church, Treasurer of the Cathedral of Cartagena, Bishop of Pampeluna—so ran the resounding titles of the offices he held, each of which contributed its flow of gold to his personal fortune. And on the day of his father's coronation he received the Archbishopric of Valenza, the premier see of Spain. The Italians, with their love of nicknames, coined a name for him from that rich gift of Valenza and called him Valentino.

The young man seems to have shared in full the easy charm of his father. The Ferrarese envoy in Rome wrote to his master:

> I met Cesare yesterday in the house in Trastevere. He was just on his way to the chase dressed in a costume altogether worldly, that is, in silk—and armed. He had only a little tonsure like a simple priest. I conversed with him ·awhile as we rode along—I am on intimate terms with him. He possesses marked genius and a charming personality, bearing himself like a great prince. He is especially lively and merry and fond of society. The archbishop never had any inclination for the priesthood—but his benefices bring him in more than 16,000 ducats annually.

Doubtless the envoy was concerned to let it be known that he was on more than nodding terms with the great, but his portrait of Cesare at the beginning of his career was borne out by other observers: a highly intelligent young man with more than sufficient charm and vigour to exploit his advantages—given the opportunity.

The opportunity did not immediately present itself, despite the fact that his father was now pope. Cesare was a student at Perugia when the election was announced, but he was not summoned to

Rome to take part in the prodigal coronation festivities which marked the beginning of the Borgia pontificate. Alexander's motive for the apparent slighting of his son was obvious. In the first consistory of his pontificate he had launched a stinging attack upon simony and nepotism and, while there was nothing he could do about the simony of his own election, he deemed it prudent to keep down the numbers of his immediate family in Rome. As a gesture to public opinion it was, naturally, a failure. 'Ten papacies would not suffice to glut this horde of relatives,' a diarist snarled on news of the benefices scattered among the Borgias immediately after the coronation. And it did nothing to reconcile Cesare to the role that had been forced upon him—particularly when the news broke that his brother Juan was about to be married to a Spanish princess while Lucrezia was herself to be married into one of the major Italian families.

Technically, Lucrezia was already married for she had exchanged vows by proxy with a minor Spanish grandee some years before her father became pope. But what was a good match for a cardinal's daughter emphatically was not good enough for the daughter of Pope Alexander VI. The contract was dissolved and Alexander looked round for a more suitable bridegroom for his daughter.

He found the bridegroom in the person of the twenty-six-year-old Giovanni Sforza, Count of Cotignola and Vicar of Pesaro. Young Sforza had no particular influence in his own right for Cotignola and Pesaro were two small towns in the Romagna and, as part of the Papal States, their feudal suzerain was the pope himself. But Sforza was connected by blood to that powerful family in Milan who controlled the gates into Italy. One of his uncles was the Duke of Milan and the other was Cardinal Ascanio Sforza, the man to whom Alexander owed his crown and who was now Vice-Chancellor, the second man in the hierarchy. It was altogether, from Alexander's point of view, an ideal match.

There was a small difficulty in that Lucrezia's discarded fiancé was not disposed to take the matter calmly, but came storming to Rome to protest. 'There is much gossip about Pesaro's marriage,' an ambassador noted. 'The first bridegroom is here, raising a great noise as Catalans do, saying he will protest to all the princes and powers of Christendom. But, willy-willy, he will have to submit.' Which was exactly what the unfortunate young man did, even binding himself not to marry for a year—just in case he was, after all, required as bridegroom.

Lucrezia was married in June 1493, in the Vatican Palace, just ten months after her father had been proclaimed pope in the same building. John Burchard, the papal master of ceremonies, recorded this curious ceremony in the Vatican with the same precise detachment that he was to record the other, and even more curious activities, of the Borgia regime. Incidentally, he gave a clear, authoritative picture of the comparatively lowly position that Cesare held in the family. It was Juan, Duke of Gandia, who escorted Lucrezia from her home to the great Sala Reale of the Vatican where, before the Throne of St Peter, the wedding was to take place. An immense train of 150 highborn Roman ladies followed her, including 'Battistina, grand-daughter of Pope Innocent VIII of blessed memory, Donna Giulia Farnese, the pope's concubine': ten cardinals flanked Alexander on his throne. 'On his left, by the wall, stood Don Cesare Borgia, the Bishop-Elect of Valenzia and another son of His Holiness, with many notables and ecclesiastics.' In that manner did Burchard, ever alert to the most subtle nuances of court etiquette, first record the eighteen-year-old youth who was merely 'another son of His Holiness'. Thereafter the Master of Ceremonies forgot Cesare in favour of recording details of the ceremony and the banqueting and dancing that followed throughout the night.

Three months afterwards, Cesare received a cardinal's hat—but so did the fifteen-year-old heir of the Duke of Ferrara and so did the debauched young brother of Giulia Farnese, the Pope's new mistress. Packing the Sacred College with friends and relatives was always a sound political manoeuvre and the hats so gained shed no particular lustre on their recipients. Cesare was now permanently in Rome, installed in one of the private apartments in the Vatican, with his own staff of servants and officials. But he still played no part in public affairs.

In a little over a year, Pope Alexander had achieved much, so far as his ambitions for his family were concerned. His eldest son was a Spanish duke, and about to be married into the royal house of Spain; his daughter was an Italian princess. He had provided even for his youngest son Joffre, betrothing the thirteen-year-old lad to the daughter of the King of Naples. But in the wider European sphere his diplomacy failed him, blinded as he was by concern for his children, and in the autumn of 1493 he encountered the supreme crisis of his career—the threat of deposition, backed by the menaces of a foreign army.

There were few, if any, moral considerations in the move to depose Alexander Borgia. It was now common knowledge that his election had been the most simoniacal on record: that the private apartments of the Vatican more closely resembled a high-class brothel than the home of a high priest of Christendom and that his one object was to advance the power of his children at no matter what cost to the Papacy. But Italians were accustomed to making the distinction between priest and monarch, and had his dynastic ambitions not conflicted with the ambitions of other Italian families, he would have been left to enjoy his pontificate in peace.

The trouble began when his enemy, Cardinal Giuliano della Rovere, fled to France and there poured into the ear of the foolish young King Charles VIII the tale of Borgia iniquity. Charles saw himself as the last of the paladins but even he would not have moved to the invasion of Italy had not certain dazzling visions been dangled before his eyes. The French had an ancient, and reasonably legitimate, claim to Naples. Let Charles enforce that claim, thereby toppling Borgia's main allies in Italy. In one campaign Charles would cleanse Christendom of the monster at its top, make himself King of Naples—and even go on to Crusade and free the Holy Places.

Charles fell for the scheme—with one proviso. The alliance of Lodovico Sforza of Milan was a prime necessity before any invasion of Italy. But even that proved simple, despite the fact that Sforza was united by marriage to the Borgia. Sforza abandoned his ally with the matter-of-fact treachery that was the hall-mark of Italian politics, for he, too, desired the overthrow of the current Neapolitan dynasty. He ruled Milan illegally, keeping the true heir safely confined. But that heir was married to a grand-daughter of the King of Naples and she had appealed to the King for aid. Willingly, therefore, Sforza allowed the French troops passage through Lombardy.

King Charles of France marched triumphantly down the peninsula, hailed throughout as the Saviour come to deliver Italy and the Church from the grip of the Borgia. But, though frightened out of his wits, Borgia survived, skilfully employing the complex, shifting alliances of Italy to confound the naive French youth. Everyone desired Alexander's deposition—but no one could agree as to who would take his place. Charles obtained a cardinal's hat for one of his favourites, and papal permission to continue the march south to the attack on Naples. That was all. Justly suspicious of any promise of Alexander's, particularly one wrung under duress, Charles insisted that Cardinal Cesare Borgia should accompany the French march south—as hostage. Alexander agreed, and it was in that humiliating role that Cesare first came into contact with the

ABOVE: The entry of Charles VIII of France into Naples 1445 (Radio Times Hulton Picture Library)

BELOW: Naples, by Pieter Brueghel (Photo Scala, Florence)

power that was to make him great. He did not long remain a hostage, but escaped a few days after the French army left Rome, evidence alike of his own resourcefulness and his captor's incompetence. The French campaign that had begun with such high hopes ended in total disaster. Naples fell easily enough but on the return northward, Charles discovered what so many other would-be conquerors had discovered in Italy—that the Italians preferred anarchy to order imposed by the most benevolent despot. His allies melted away and either remained neutral or joined Alexander, launching attack after attack upon the demoralized French until the mauled army at last reached the safety of the Alps and home.

The French invasion had achieved none of its long-term objects. Instead, it had fatally disturbed what peace there remained in Italy and it was Pope Alexander and his family who profited from the discord. It was easy to show that the enemies of Borgia were also the enemies of Italy, and Alexander was able to begin the task of eliminating them, secure in the knowledge that he had the tacit support of most Italians. Juan, Duke of Gandia, was summoned from Spain to lead the papal armies against the rebellious nobles who had dared align themselves with France. His father invested him with the territories of those he was about to despoil, creating him Prince of Teano and Tricarico, Duke of Benevento and Terracina, Gonfaloniere of the Holy Church, and, blessing him, sent him off on Holy War.

But his brother Cesare remained merely Cardinal-Deacon of Santa Maria Nuova, neither a layman nor a fully-fledged priest, passing his time between hunting and bullfighting and carousing. So it was thought.

2. Duke Valentino

Duke Valentino, by Raphael (Mansell Collection)

Vanozza Catanei had followed the careers of her children with the liveliest interest. Alexander had removed them from her care while they were still very young—for what reason the world never knew—but he never attempted to deny her access to them. She was in the background now, first overshadowed by the new mistress Giulia Farnese, and then by the growing splendour of her own children. But the bond between them still remained very strong.

As with all the family, save Cesare, she was delighted with the honours heaped upon her eldest son Juan and on the evening of Wednesday, 14 June 1497, she gave a dinner party in his honour and to wish him godspeed before his departure in quest of military glory. Cesare, too, was invited. The party took place in the vineyard of her home in Rome and was a sober, decorous affair as befitted a respected Roman matron. The guests were all relatives or close friends of the family and the party broke up at a comparatively early hour.

Cesare and Juan left together, accompanied by a few servants, and rode back to the Vatican. Before they reached it Juan took leave of his brother, saying in effect that the night was still young and other pleasures awaited him. He took with him only a footman and a man in a festive mask who had been his constant companion over the past month. He was never seen alive again.

On the following morning the Duke's servants reported to Alexander that their master had not yet returned home. Alexander, though alarmed, comforted himself with the thought that Juan had probably spent the night with a woman and was reluctant to leave her house in daylight. But when night came and the Duke was still absent he gave orders that a rigorous search was to be mounted.

The footman who had been with the Duke was found, mortally wounded. The only information he could give was that the Duke had dismissed him and had ridden off with his drinking companion mounted on the crupper of his mule. He was apparently incapable of saying when or where he was himself attacked.

During the course of the search, the papal officials happened to question a timber-merchant who was keeping watch on his yard from a boat on the river. In reply to their question as to whether he had noticed anything particular the night before, he told a detailed story of how a group of men had brought a body to the river and thrown it in near the sewage outfall. Asked why he had not reported the matter he replied that, in his time, he had seen a hundred bodies thrown into the river near the point: no one had ever troubled to question him about them and he had seen no particular importance in this incident.

A massive dredging operation was immediately put in hand and, late on the afternoon of the following day, the body of Juan was dragged up from the approximate area that the timber-merchant had indicated. It was fully clad: even his gloves were still tucked into a belt which contained thirty ducats, a large enough sum to tempt any robber. The body bore nine terrible wounds, one in his neck and the others over his head, body and legs.

Such was the account of the murder of the Duke of Gandia which John Burchard committed to his private diary. He, of all people, was in the best position to know the identity of the murderer if that knowledge were even whispered in the papal court. The nature of his duties brought him into contact with all the major figures in Rome, including the ambassadors of foreign powers, and sooner or later most secrets of state came to the ears of this discreet and colourless man. But he knew nothing regarding the identity of the murderer and, ever preferring facts to rumours, contented himself with an exact account of the murder itself.

There were rumours in plenty to choose. Prime favourite at first was the young Giovanni Sforza, the unfortunate husband of Lucrezia. The change in political alignment had destroyed his value to the Borgia and he had been forcibly divorced from Lucrezia on the shameful grounds of impotence. But though he had motive, he had no opportunity, Rome being far too dangerous a place for him.

Rumour next alighted on Sforza's uncle, Cardinal Ascanio Sforza, the one time friend and ally of Alexander. But he, too, had fallen from favour as a result of the French invasion and had thought it wiser to quit Rome. He was unperturbed by the accusation, and gave it as his opinion that the murder had been personal, not political, and that Juan had fallen victim to an enraged husband.

The great Roman family of the Orsini came under obvious suspicion. They, too, had been allies of the Borgia, had unwisely aligned themselves with the French and were then forced to watch while Juan set about sequestering their territories at the orders of his father.

And finally there was the dead man's brother, Cesare. It was not until a year after the murder that the accusations were first made and then by men who, unlike Burchard, were not privy to papal secrets and were not even in Rome at the time of the murder. The motives ascribed to him were various and colourful. The most popular was that he and Juan were rivals for the affection of their brother Joffre's wife, Donna Sancia. It was an unlikely accusation for Donna Sancia dispensed her favours pretty freely around Rome and it would have been both ludicrous and lethal for any one lover to resent the activities of others.

A vicious twist was later given to the story by substituting Lucrezia's name for Sancia's, making Cesare and Juan the rivals in an incestuous love affair. That particular rumour stemmed straight back to Lucrezia's divorced husband, Giovanni Sforza. Enraged by the humiliating official judgement that the marriage was rendered null by his impotence, he had burst out with the startling statement that the real reason why Alexander wanted the divorce was because he wanted to enjoy his daughter himself. The accusation was totally unsubstantiated, and made under stress by a young man forced to witness the sudden collapse of a brilliant career in addition to enduring the mockery of a cruel society. But it was taken up joyfully by the increasing number of enemies of the Borgia and embroidered without limit, making Alexander the rival of both his sons for his daughter's favours, one of whom eventually murdered the other.

The most damaging accusation against Cesare was that he

murdered his brother in order to take his place as Duke of Gandia. Even the sketchiest knowledge of the laws of inheritance would have convinced Cesare of the pointlessness of such an attempt for the Dukedom would naturally be inherited—as it was in fact—by Juan's eldest son. But there was nothing inherently improbable in the charge. Cesare later demonstrated clearly enough that he accepted private murder, as well as public war, as a necessary continuance of politics and the fact that his brother Juan was monopolizing the secular honours of the family at his expense might have been motive enough. But no direct proof of his guilt was ever unearthed and the probability was that Juan's murder, as Ascanio Sforza surmised, was 'something to do with a love affair'. It was a reasonable surmise, based on a knowledge of Juan's amorous habits and the fact that he had been killed not cleanly, as by an assassin, but in an apparent frenzy of hatred as the numerous wounds on a helpless man bore evidence.

Alexander was shattered by the news of the murder. It had been upon Juan that his far-reaching hopes for a dynasty were based and his first reaction was typically extreme. After the initial passion of his grief was spent, he summoned a solemn Consistory and there swore that he would reform both himself and the Church. Simony and nepotism were alike to be purged and, to show his intention, he even banished Lucrezia and Donna Sancia from Rome. But it was a short-lived determination: a number of minor clergy were punished for breaches of canon law but a few weeks after the Consistory the Borgia family were back in Rome as though nothing had ever happened.

Cesare might have been innocent of Juan's murder but he immediately profited from it in the one manner that he desired. Alexander was forced to employ his second son as instrument of his policy in the secular field. Just a month after the murder, Cesare was sent on a mission to the rebellious papal cities in Umbria. He went as cardinal, with only a small escort, and he achieved much despite his protest that it was useless to attempt to subdue rebels by persuasion only. 'It is vital to provide me with an army against these demons,' he wrote to his father. 'Holy water won't banish them.' But Alexander still clung to the hope that Cesare would follow him in the Church and declined to invest him with any military authority. Nevertheless Cesare continued his tour of the disaffected cities, showing remarkably courage and skill considering his total lack of military experience and the tiny police force at his command. In Perugia he even dared to expel the powerful ringleaders—and was obeyed. The Perugians, it seemed, were overjoyed at the sudden appearance of law and order in the shape of the young cardinal. 'I captured two robbers and murderers—and there was no tumult,' he reported to Rome. 'To the delight of the people they were put in prison—a thing long unknown in this city—and this morning I hanged one.'

The brief taste of power urged Cesare on to his immediate ambition—the total renunciation of his priestly role in favour of becoming the secular champion of the Borgia. It gave him, too, an additional argument with which to try to sway his father. He had been tested in the field and emerged with credit—which was more than could be said for the military exploits of the late Duke of Gandia. Alexander wavered. In February 1498 rumours abounded in Rome that Cesare was about to renounce his cardinalate. There were hints of a royal marriage for him with a daughter of the house of Naples. In Venice it was whispered that Lucrezia, too, was on the marriage market, that the whole policy of the Borgias was taking on a new complexion.

But still Alexander declined to exercise his power and rid Cesare of a distasteful burden. Even though he was convinced that his son would be a worthy successor to Juan, there was one great problem which stayed Alexander's hand. The bulk of Cesare's income came from the Church: if he were to renounce his hat, he would be rendered a poor man, as far as the Borgia accounted poverty. And so matters stood unsatisfactorily throughout the spring and early summer of 1498.

The solution came from an unexpected source—the same French monarchy which, four years earlier, had set out to topple the Borgia régime. But matters had changed in France. The fantastic young Charles VIII was dead, Louis XII ruled in his stead, and Louis urgently desired dispensation from his present marriage in order to marry again—more advantageously. His ministers approached the only person who could give this dispensation, Pope Alexander VI. And Alexander let it be known that the dispensation would indeed be forthcoming, provided that King Louis could see his way clear to provide Cesare Borgia with a suitable estate. In his turn, Louis replied that he would be delighted to do this, and would invest Cesare with the Dukedom of Valentinois in the Dauphiné— provided, of course, that he was a layman.

Now, rapidly, the complex Borgia manoeuvrings bore public fruit. Lucrezia was, indeed, on the verge of a new marriage—to the nephew of the King of Naples. But even her marriage was to be only a stepping stone for her brother. Cesare himself was to marry the King's daughter, Carlotta, and so move directly into the line of the Neapolitan succession.

Such was the intention, but it received an apparent check when the King announced that his daughter had no desire to marry 'a priest and the son of a priest'. Carlotta's objection seems to have been genuine even though her father's was purely political, based on a wholesome dislike of being too closely linked to the Borgia. From his point of view, it would have been challenging fate to admit a third Borgia into his house, particularly one with the growing reputation that Cesare had acquired.

By now, Alexander had obviously accepted the fact that Cesare's place was in the outside world. On 13 August 1498, the twenty-two-year-old cardinal arose in his last Consistory and begged his brethren leave to renounce his sacred office. The Sacred College accepted his loss with equanimity but the Spanish ambassador afterwards protested vigorously to Alexander. It was now common knowledge that the Spanish ex-cardinal was about to become a French Duke, owing allegiance to an enemy of Spain. But Alexander squashed the objection with the unanswerable remark that it was necessary for Cesare's spiritual well-being.

Clearly, now, the change in Borgia policy was becoming apparent. Hitherto, Alexander had exerted all his efforts to establish his dynasty in the country of his origin—Spain—and to maintain the best possible relationship with the Spanish house that now ruled Naples. France was becoming the great friend and ally and to foster that alliance the Borgia were prepared to weaken their links with their native land. Cesare was the poorer by some 35,000 ducats annually—but almost immediately he had received the letters patent from Louis that made him Duke of Valentinois, with an income of 20,000 francs per year. A net loss was shown, but very rapidly Cesare transformed it into profit.

Cesare left for France three months after his renunciation of the purple. It was his first major mission on behalf of his father. Certain high matters of state were to be discussed with the French monarch, matters whose delicacy could not be entrusted to any save a Borgia. But, in addition, Cesare had a personal object in going to France. The matter of the Neapolitan princess had still not been resolved. The desired bride, Carlotta, was in residence at the French court and both Cesare and his father felt, reasonably enough, that King Louis would be more than willing to bring pressure to bear on the girl when he had learned what the Borgia could do for him.

Cesare left Rome on 1 October 1498. Even as cardinal, he had never been noted for sobriety in custume and display, and his ambassadorial equipage would have done honour to a king. Alexander watched the procession leave, standing at a window of the Vatican and bursting with pride and pleasure. Whatever reluctance he had felt in allowing Cesare to adopt a secular career was now totally forgotten and, from henceforth, Cesare was first charge upon his loyalty, his pride and his purse. 'The Duke is Our heart, Our favourite son, who is prized by Us beyond all else,' was the burden of the letter of credentials that Cesare carried, together with the coveted dispensation and a cardinal's hat for one of Louis's favourites.

French galleys took the papal party from Civita Vecchia to Marseilles and from there they rode on to Avignon. The City Fathers had borrowed heavily to put on a suitable welcome for the Duke of Valentinois, although they were hampered by the fact that there was no precedence to guide them in entertaining the son of a pope. They solved the problem, correctly, by assuming that the entertainment he desired would be that befitting a young and wealthy Italian prince.

> The streets of the town from Porte St Lazare, where he will enter, to the Petit Palace shall be decorated with hangings and in the streets there shall be merriments and plays, with divers games. A rich and beautiful gift of silver plate shall be made to the said Don Cesare and, finally, that no expression of joy be wanting, he shall be feted in the Maison de la Ville with ladies and beautiful girls, for the said lord Don Cesare takes much pleasure therein, knowing well how to entertain them.

The Avignonese preparations obviously came up to Cesare's standard for, instead of continuing his journey on to where the king was waiting at Chinon, he remained in Avignon for the better part of a month. The Avignonese were accustomed to splendour: their city had been the seat of the Papacy not so long before, earning for itself a European reputation for the corruption that sprang from its inordinate luxury, but even they were astounded by the prodigality of Cesare's display. He himself seems to have been looked upon as though he were some rare animal. Wherever he moved, crowds followed, watching every movement of this representative of a family which had already acquired an awesome reputation. A member of his entourage wrote home to say that they had seen nothing of trees and houses in France, nothing but people pressing round and the sunlight overhead.

By early December Cesare had had his fill of Avignonese entertainment and continued on to Chinon, arriving there in the middle of the month. Deliberately, he planned an ostentatious entry into the town. The lengthy file of heavily laden sumpter mules that led the cavalcade were expensively decked out in his colours of scarlet and yellow, each animal conspicuously bearing the Borgia crest of the Bull and Cesare's own insignia of the Flame. Sixteen gentlemen of his court followed on horses caparisoned, in the Spanish manner, with towering cockades of gold and furnished with silver bridles and stirrups. Behind them came twenty mounted pages, dressed in crimson velvet or cloth of gold and finally came Cesare himself, surrounded by sixty gentlemen of his personal staff. Scattered throughout the cavalcade were musicians and immediately preceding the duke was a corps of eight trumpeters.

Cesare appeared in a blaze of jewels. His basic costume was the curiously sombre black velvet that he was afterwards to adopt habitually but on this occasion it was slashed to show the gold brocade of the undergarment. Gold caparisoned his suberb warhorse—gold beaten out into thin leaves: even its tail was confined in a net of gold worked with pearls. Gold buttons, each with a great ruby in the centre, fastened the duke's doublet. Pearls and more rubies were in his hat and on his boots, diamonds flashed upon his breast. The overall effect was more barbaric than magnificent, the costume of a parvenu. Designed to impress, it merely aroused the contempt of the King. Watching the display from his castle window he sneered: 'It is too much for the petty Duke of Valentinois.'

Louis was friendly enough when they met, willing to overlook the pretensions of an upstart for the sake of the advantages he represented. Cordially he received permission to marry the woman he had already married; cordially he received the cardinal's hat for George d'Amboise. In the prevailing fraternal atmosphere he was even able to bring about a reconciliation between Giuliano della Rovere, still a refugee at his court, and the son of Giuliano's enemy.

But then rapidly the atmosphere cooled as the result of an unexpected setback. Everyone, including Louis, had assumed that a simple word from him would bring the Princess Carlotta to her senses. She was, after all, a lady in his wife's entourage and was accustomed to doing as she was told. But now that she had actually seen the bridegroom proposed for her Carlotta was, if anything, even more adamant. She would *not* marry Cesare and that was that.

Della Rovere, anxious to ingratiate himself with Alexander, gave the news in a conciliatory letter. It was not Cesare's fault: 'By his modesty, his readiness, his prudence and his other virtues he has gained everyone's affections. The young lady, however, either through sheer perversity—or because she has been influenced by others, which is easier to believe—absolutely declines to hear of the wedding.' Alexander refused to be conciliated. In a furious letter to the cardinal he declared that he had been made a laughing stock. 'All Europe was very well aware that, but for the French king's plain promise to find a wife for him, Cesare would have remained in Italy.'

In France, Cesare took his rebuff with a bad grace. He sulked, declined to discuss those high matters which Louis so greatly desired to discuss and eventually announced that he intended to return home forthwith. In desperation, Louis thought of another expediency— the provision of a substitute bride.

In his wife's entourage there was another princess being brought up, according to the custom of the day, at a foreign court. She was Charlotte d'Albret, daughter of Alain, Duke of Guyenne, and sister of the King of Navarre. Socially, she was a fitting match for Cesare, related as she was to the French royal house. She was, and remained, a pawn moving briefly from obscurity to fame and then once more to obscurity. Few, therefore, troubled to record their impressions of her but, dimly through the sparse conventional flatteries, can be divined a rather attractive girl—deeply religious, but not fanatically so, sweet-tempered, gentle and accounted beautiful. Charlotte, at seventeen years of age, was not the obvious match for Cesare Borgia, but the negotiations, surprisingly, were crowned with rapid success.

It was the cupidity of Charlotte's father which brought about the result. Alain d'Albret was at once penurious and avaricious. He knew, as everyone knew, of the humilation that the Borgia suffered and promptly placed a fantastically high price upon his daughter. The pope was to endow her with 100,000 ducats. His own dowry of 90,000 ducats cost him nothing for it was Charlotte's inheritance from her mother—and it was, in any case, to be used only for purchasing a suitable estate in France, not Italy.

His preliminary proposals were accepted so swiftly that he promptly squeezed harder. He demanded, in addition, a cardinal's hat for his son. The proposal was carried to Cesare who immediately promised the hat on behalf of his father. Even Alain was satisfied and the bargain was struck. The marriage contract was signed on 10 May 1499 and two days later Cesare and Chalotte were married with the minimum of ceremony.

The high matters of state at last could be discussed between Louis and Cesare. The marriage contract stated very clearly why King

Louis had gone to such extraordinary lengths to placate Cesare with a royal bride.

> The said lord [Louis] having been made duly acquainted with the great and commendable services which the high and mighty prince Don Coesar de Boursa has rendered to him and his crown—and which he trusts that the said duke, his relations, friends and allies shall render in time to come, likewise touching the conquest of his kingdoms of Naples and Duchy of Milan . . . [has] agreed upon the said marriage.

Louis was planning another French invasion of Italy and needed, above all, the firm support of the Borgia clan.

Louis's claims to the kingdom of Naples and the duchy of Milan were at least as good as those of their present rulers. Two centuries earlier his Angevine ancestors had conquered Naples, to be dispossessed, in 1442, by the current Spanish house. He claimed Milan on the grounds that he was a lineal descendant of its first legitimate duke, who had died 150 years before. He intended to repossess himself of his inheritances—Milan first, and then Naples.

Louis's claims were, legally, unobjectionable. But the plan to plunge all Italy into bloody turmoil in order to implement dusty title deeds could have succeeded only because of the fratricidal jealousy of the Italian city-states. A unified front would have stopped the catastrophic invasion before it had passed the Alps. But unity was impossible, each petty prince believing that he, personally, would survive the holocaust with his powers augmented.

Such was the plan which Louis put before Cesare, plenipotentiary of the Roman pontiff. It meant throwing the Sforza allies of the Borgia, finally, to the wolves of France. It meant the abandoning of that Neapolitan house into which Cesare had so recently been trying to marry himself. It meant that, if successful, the inimical power of France would be established permanently in the north and the south of Italy. Cesare agreed to the plan, with one proviso. As soon as Milan had been captured, the military machine of France should be placed at his disposal so that he could carve himself a principality in Italy. Louis accepted the proviso.

There were a few legal and ceremonial matters to be settled now that the major agreement had been made. Louis was invested with his dukedom of Valentinois, entitled now to call himself 'Caesar Borgia of France' and quarter the Lilies with the Bull of his arms. Curiously, the Italian version of Valentinois was the same as for his quondam archbishopric of Valenza, so that he still remained Valentino on Italian tongues. Louis formally enrolled him in his army with a stipend of 20,000 francs per year in addition to the income he drew from his duchy. But his standard of living in France was such that Italy still had to subsidize his splendour. Alexander gladly found the money—32,000 ducats of it: 'to send to France where the Duke of Valentinois is living at great expense—and this money was over and above what he took with him', the papal treasurer recorded.

Alexander was delighted with the news from France. Privately he had admitted to an ambassador 'that he had entertained strong doubts as to the marriage taking place but now that it was concluded, he was pleased, and whereas he used to speak evil of France, he was now all French for the love the King of France had shown towards his Duke'. There was talk of finding more money to bring Charlotte to Rome—the girl had already written saying how she longed to come and pay her respects to her father-in-law, adding, with an engaging touch of humour, that she was 'very well satisfied with the Duke'—but that particular project never bore fruit.

In September, a massive French army overwhelmed Milan, Duke Lodovico Sforza flying after the flimsiest opposition. At the end of the month, Cesare left France with the king to make the ceremonial entry into Milan. Charlotte d'Albret, pregnant with her first child, never saw her husband again.

Siege of Milan, by Vasari (Photo Scala, Florence)

3. The States of the Church

Florence, by Vasari (Photo Scala, Florence)

Eight centuries before, a scribe in the papal Chancery had forged a document which affected the course of Italian history for a thousand years and now, incidentally, provided the base for the empire of Cesare Borgia. The forgery was lengthy, complex and skilful: its gist was that the Emperor Constantine, on his conversion to Christianity, had ceded all the Western World to the Bishop of Rome and his descendants in perpetuity.

Armed with this document, successive popes persuaded successive emperors to honour the gift of their great predecessor and cede part, at least, of their Italian possessions to St Peter. Haphazardly over the centuries, the Papal States grew until, in 1500, they consisted of a broad belt, running across the entire peninsula from north-east to south-west.

The so-called Donation of Constantine had long been exposed for the impudent forgery that it was, but the Papal States had rooted themselves too deeply to be uprooted. They were a fact of geography, bisecting Italy. In theory, the papal monarch was the absolute lord of this huge bloc. In practice, the papal cities were ruled by vicars owing more or less allegiance to the pope, depending upon their power. It was in the Papal States that the practice of nepotism had achieved its extreme and most damaging form. The gift of a papal office to a 'nephew' could be rescinded by a stroke of the pen of the next pontiff. The gift of a papal city could be revoked only by a bloody struggle. Most of the present so-called vicars were descendants of 'nephews' of earlier popes—descendants who, by the sheer force of possession, had turned a granted office into an hereditary possession.

Alexander, therefore, was establishing no remarkable precedent, nor being particularly unjust, when he decided to oust some of the reigning vicars and install his son in their stead. Unusual, perhaps, was the cynicism of his pretext and the scale of the envisaged expulsions. Ten cities in the northern provinces of the States, most of them in Romagna, were marked down as Cesare's prey and a papal bull was published declaring that, because the vicars had fallen behind in their feudal dues, their fiefs were now escheated to the Roman Church. One of the vicars, the formidable Caterina Sforza of Forli, promptly sent her envoys to prove, conclusively, that far from being in debt to the Holy See, she was some 60,000 ducats in advance of payment. It made not the slightest difference.

On 7 November 1499 King Louis left Milan for France and, two days later, Cesare rode out of the city at the head of the army lent to him by Louis. It was a compact force of some 7,000 veteran Swiss and Gascons—mostly foot but with a strong stiffening of cavalry and artillery. Together with the 3,000 troops being assembled for him in Romagna by papal commissioners it was more than adequate for the task that lay ahead. For the problems that faced Cesare at the outset of his campaign were less military than political. Romagna was ringed around by independent states, each of them jealously watching Cesare though each, for different reasons, was prepared to acquiesce in the destruction of the Romagnols. In the north lay the most menacing of them all—the Most Serene Republic of Venice—an island empire with an immensely strong navy, invulnerable to land attack, wealthy, and able to draw upon allies scattered around Italy. The Venetians had very few territorial ambitions in Italy: all they desired was to create a buffer between

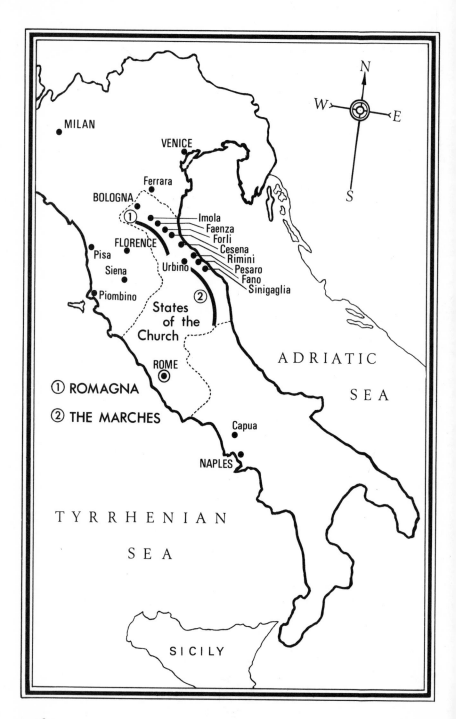

themselves and their turbulent fellow Italians. It was for this reason that they had allied themselves with Louis of France, in order to destroy their Sforza neighbour.

To the south lay the growing Rupublic of Florence, uneasy lord over half a dozen once powerful, independent cities of whom Arezzo and Pisa were permanently on the brink of revolt. Far more vulnerable than Venice, Florence presented an even trickier problem to Cesare. The Florentines, too, were allies of Louis of France—and had had the good sense to stiffen that alliance with Florentine gold. 40,000 ducats went annually into Louis's pockets, a sufficient guarantee of his loyalty.

In between these two major states were a handful of semi-independent princes of whom the Este in Ferrara and Gonzaghi in Mantua were the most powerful.

Cesare, therefore, was in the position of a man advancing down an uncertainly marked path through a minefield. If he strayed too far on one side, then Venice would infallibly explode in his face. If he strayed on the other, then there could be a far greater explosion from France, turning an utterly essential ally into an enemy.

The immediate future, however, presented few problems for his first victim was a woman whom no one cared to defend. Caterina Sforza was Cesare's female counterpart, the first woman, perhaps, to earn the equivocal compliment of being dubbed 'virago'. At thirty-seven she was still a beauty, a highly intelligent, widely-read woman of no scruples whatsoever. She ruled the cities of Forli and Imola as heiress of her husband, Girolamo Riario, who had been granted them by his uncle Pope Sixtus. After Riario's inevitable assassination she had married, in an advanced state of pregnancy, her lover Giovanni de' Medici and after his death added two more lovers to her list, both of whom were butchered in rebellions. She put down the rebellions, and avenged both her husband and her lovers, in an ecstasy of savagery. Her subjects hated, but feared her. They still told the story of how on the day before she gave birth to a child, she had mounted horse, ridden miles and smashed an incipient act of treachery by a castellan.

Related by marriage to a powerful Florentine family, and by birth to the Milanese dynasty, she had been supremely confident of her ability to repel the Borgia threat. But Milan fell at a touch and the Florentines, following their ancient policy of 'wait and see', limited their aid to comforting words. Venice was against her—and whomsoever Venice was against was doomed.

Secure in the knowledge that he had a clear field, Cesare advanced upon the first city in his line of march, Caterina's subject city of Imola. The town did not so much surrender as rush out and welcome the invader. The governor withdrew with his garrison to the castle and there held out gallantly enough for two weeks. Then, running short of supplies he informed, honourably, Caterina at Forli that he must surrender if no reinforcements came. No reinforcements came and he surrendered. He was a fortunate man: Caterina did not execute his children whom she held as hostage and Cesare, anxious to make a good impression, did not execute him.

In a little over three weeks after leaving Milan, Cesare had achieved his first military victory. Two weeks later he had achieved his second when, on 19 December, he entered Forli to the cheers of the people. Then came the first opposition.

Caterina Sforza was a tyrant, but she was also a very brave and determined woman. She had shown evidence of that at the very beginning when, learning that the Borgia had resolved on her destruction, she resolved to remove the dynamo of their power, Pope Alexander VI himself. She sent him a letter that had been placed on the corpse of a plague victim. The weapon so created was considerably more effective than the famed Borgia poison, already achieving the realm of legend, and would probably have solved many Italian problems had it come into contact with Alexander. But the plot was discovered, the envoys executed and the letter burnt in its protective wooden cannister.

The city of Forli had fallen, but Caterina was safe in its immensely strong fortress and no city could be deemed taken until its fort was captured. This fortress had been built long before the days of fire-arms, but it had been skilfully adapted so that artillery could be employed in its defence.

Cesare's advance from Imola had been so rapid that his artillery was still lumbering on its way through the mountain passes. There was little that could be done until it arrived—except to pretend to negotiate and Caterina was far too wily to be caught with the most honeyed Borgia promises.

Meanwhile, the brief honeymoon between the invaders and the citizens of Forli was over. Cesare's troops were for the most part foreigners and to them, Forli was merely another captured foreign city. Rape, murder, extortion, destruction: this was the normal coin with which the French paid their defeated enemies and it was the coin which the Forlivesi received. The citizens appealed to Cesare but there was little he could do: his troops were answerable only to the absent King of France. In addition, as supplies dwindled during

Cesare Borgia in Palazzo Venezia, Rome, artist unknown (Photo Scala. Florence)

Caterina Sforza, by Marco Palmezzani (Mansell Collection)

that miserably cold winter, the citizens were forced to dig ever deeper into their scanty stocks to feed the invader. And, meanwhile, the besieging troops heard sounds of laughter and music from the fortress.

On Christmas Day, Cesare received an unpleasant surprise. As the wan dawn-light strengthened it was seen that a new banner was flying from the castle ramparts, a banner apparently bearing the crouching winged lion of the Republic of Venice. To the watchers, it could mean only one thing—that the Republic of Venice had changed its enigmatic mind, that Caterina Sforza was now under its protection, and that the future of Cesare Borgia was extremely dubious. Cesare hastened in person to the Venetian envoy present with his army and there received the welcome assurance that Venice had not changed sides, and that the banner, in fact, was not the Lion of St Mark. A more careful inspection showed that it was the rather similar standard of Bologna, and it was later learned that a Bolognese in the garrison had hauled it up on his own initiative.

By December 28th, Cesare's artillery was in position and for the next two weeks kept up a continual bombardment. Siege artillery had the advantage over the defence in that it could concentrate upon one section of the wall, and this was the tactic that Cesare employed. Time was now running very short. Rumours abounded that Lodovico Sforza, the late Duke of Milan, was planning a return—and if that happened, Cesare's troops would be withdrawn immediately for the defence of Milan.

On 12 January an enormous section of the wall fell into the moat. Immediately, soldiers embarked on rafts already prepared and crossed over. Even then, the fort should not have fallen. The gap was strongly covered by guns ready loaded—guns which could have mowed down the defenceless men on the rafts. But someone forgot to give the order and the breach was taken. By nightfall the fighting, conducted with a terrible savagery, was over and Caterina was a prisoner. By an accident that proved supremely fortunate for her, the man who arrested her was a Frenchman. French military law forbade the taking of women as prisoners-of-war: technically, she was now under the protection of King Louis—a fact which ultimately saved her life.

It did not save her from Cesare. His later reputation as rapist was on a par with his later reputation as poisoner—a stratum of fact raised into a mountain of legend by writers eager at once to titillate and appal. Some of his legendary exploits would have done credit to Hercules. He defended himself once from a charge of

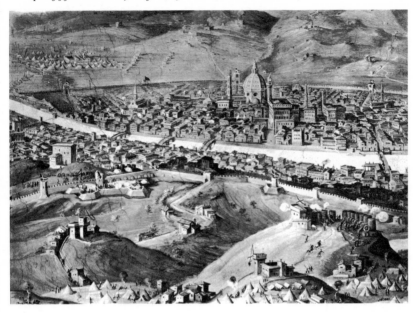

abduction with the reasonable remark that he did not usually find women so reluctant that he must needs employ rape. It was a reasonable remark for he had inherited that charm of his father's which, a hostile diarist recorded, attracted women 'as a magnet attracts iron'. But Caterina had fallen to him as spoil of war, and her total violation, personal as well as political, happily combined pleasure with a political objective—the degradation of an opponent. So, at least her late subjects thought, briefly forgetting their own misery while contemplating 'the great cruelties inflicted on our unhappy lady, Caterina Sforza, who had such a beautiful body'. For the first time ever known, Caterina lost her nerve, shrieking and fighting when, after a brief period of refuge while Cesare and the French disputed her possession, she was dragged back to his quarters.

The capture of Forli came not a moment too soon. Ten days afterwards, moving with his habitual swiftness Cesare was *en route* to his next victim—the State of his ex-brother-in-law Giovanni Sforza. But before the siege of Pesaro could begin, news came that the Sforza Duke of Milan had raised troops in his exile and was marching on the city. It was made very clear that Cesare's power, at the moment, was at the mercy of France. The troops under his command were immediately withdrawn and his campaign came instantly to a halt. There was nothing to do but return to Rome and wait.

Apart from a brief private visit to his father during the summer, Cesare had not returned to Rome since he had left it for France fourteen months earlier. His entry was accordingly magnificent, a Roman triumph in the old style. The task of organizing the procession fell to John Burchard—a thankless task, judging by the tight-lipped entry in his diary, for the mixed national groups that formed Cesare's command jostled for precedence and even fought among each other. An additional complication was rendered by the fact that Alexander had ordered all the cardinals, with their households, to ride out and welcome his Duke and there was more trouble about precedence between these and the attending ambassadors of foreign powers.

But at last it was sorted out and at midday on Wednesday, 26 February Cesare entered the city he had left as an unfrocked priest. He did not repeat the mistake of Chinon and appear in ostentatious personal splendour. He was dressed simply, almost severely, in black. Black, too, was the costume of the hundred men who formed his personal body-guard, their sombre dress accentuating their master's eminence among the parti-coloured blaze of colour that was the costume of all other men. Gossip later spread that Caterina was in the procession, bound with golden chains. But Burchard knew nothing of this, and it is probable that a prisoner in whom the French were already showing lively interest was discreetly hustled away.

Alexander received his son in the great throne-room called the Pappagallo. What passed between father and son remained a secret for, though he apparently strained to listen, Burchard could not understand their conversation for they spoke in Spanish. But that Alexander exulted in his son's success his attitude in the following months made abundantly clear.

Cesare became the effective lord of Rome—the arbiter of the ancient city, the controller of the temporal Papacy. Of that there is little doubt. The edicts which governed the city went out on his approval or at his direct instigation. The creation of cardinals was at his disposal. He made this quite clear in the July of that year when twelve cardinals were created, contributing a total of 120,000 ducats to the papal treasury—ducats which immediately made their way into the Borgia coffers. Smoothly, he addressed the College, hoping that the cardinals were content with the creation of new cardinals in order that he could have money for the enterprise in Romagna. Alexander confirmed that some time later when a disappointed ecclesiastic protested because he had not been placed on the list. Cesare drew up the list, Alexander replied with what appears to be a hint of wryness, of apology. It had nothing to do with him. What means Cesare employed to gain ascendancy over the tough old man was never certain. Initially, it arose from Alexander's overweening pride and love for his family. In a vivid pen portrait of the pope at that time the Venetian ambassador Capello reported: 'The pope is seventy years old—but grows younger every day. His cares do not last a night. His only thought is for the aggrandizement of his children—he troubles himself about nothing else.'

Cesare had amply justified his choice of career and Alexander would deny nothing to a son who was manifestly bringing such glory to the Borgia name. It was natural, too, that a vigorous, intelligent young man of twenty-four should shoulder increasingly the burdens of an old man. Alexander by no means abdicated power. It was he who planned the grand strategy, sometimes even in opposition to Cesare's immediate desires and, at such times, it was usually Cesare who gave way. But to most observers it appeared that Duke Valentino was now the head of the Borgia clan, directing it towards a still secret goal.

The check in the Romagna campaign caused by the withdrawal of French troops was no more than an irritating delay—a delay, moreover, which proved valuable. Success had followed success with an almost embarassing swiftness and, during the nine months that Cesare remained in Rome, father and son were able to plan far-reaching policies. In April came news that the fox of Milan had doubled on his last tracks: Lodovico Sforza's attempt to regain his dukedom ended in disaster. He was conducted to a prison in France, there to spin out the remaining ten years of his life in despair, and shortly afterwards French envoys came to Rome anxious to refurbish the Borgia alliance. Louis would again put his troops at Cesare's disposal, provided that the Borgia assisted him in his forthcoming attack on Naples.

The French proposals for the dismemberment of Naples created a touch of embarrassment in that Lucrezia's Neapolitan husband, the Duke of Bisceglie, was even then present in Rome. Until now, Lucrezia had acquiesced passively in her role of pawn, first accepting with equanimity an Italian instead of a Spanish husband and then accepting the bizarre farrago of the legal process which pronounced null her marriage with Giovanni Sforza. Rumour had it, indeed, that she had conspired with Cesare to frighten the wretched young man from Rome.

But the breaking of her relationship with her present husband Bisceglie was another matter entirely. At twenty, she knew her own mind—so far as she was capable—and was undoubtedly deeply in love with him. Her later actions showed that unequivocally. Moreover, she was now the mother of a six-month-old boy, a possible heir to the Neapolitan kingdom: maternal pride and wifely love combined presented a formidable obstacle to the plans of her brother and, presumably, those of her father.

Cesare destroyed the obstacle by direct action: such was the considered opinion of Rome when, on July 15th it was learned that Alfonso, Duke of Bisceglie, was lying mortally wounded, the victim of a murderous attack. Paolo Capello, the Venetian ambassador, sent his principals a detailed report in which he specifically accused Cesare as the murderer. Bisceglie, he wrote, was attacked on the steps of St Peter's and stabbed by an unidentified gang. He was able to stagger to the Vatican and, for nearly a month, was nursed by Lucrezia. She, it seemed, feared that an attempt would be made to finish him off with poison.

According to the same source Alexander, too, had fears for his son-in-law's safety and ordered that a permanent guard of sixteen men should be mounted near the sick chamber. Given the correctness of his suspicion that Cesare was the power behind the attempted assassination, the guard was less than useless. Cesare visited the wounded man and was credited with the remark, made presumably as he left that, 'That which did not take place at noon will take place in the evening'.

On 18 August, Bisceglie was strangled in his bed. The actual murderer was Michelotto, the Spaniard now widely known as Cesare's executioner, but Cesare was present, having first driven away his sister and her women and, again presumably, dismissed the guard.

Capello's story, though circumspect and full of detail, contained a bewildering number of lacunae and contradictions. But the sober Burchard confirmed the important facts—the striking down of Bisceglie and his death by violence nearly a month later. He did not identify the murderer by name. Admittedly, his diary was private, but private papers easily passed into other hands and Burchard was, above all, a professional survivor. At the end of his bald account he stated simply that the investigation had been closed by orders from above—for the man behind the act was well known. There was only one man in Rome who could have been known to commit such a deed and yet escape the consequences.

It is perhaps from this point onwards that Cesare began his dominance over his father. Capello ended his report with a curious

Lucrezia Borgia, by Pinturicchio (Mansell Collection)

phrase: 'The pope loves and has great fear of his son the duke.' The love Alexander had for Cesare was of the same quality that he had had for the late Duke of Gandia, the love arising from family vanity. But he did, undoubtedly, love Lucrezia in a deeply personal manner. Although the murder of Bisceglie fitted in neatly enough with his overall plans, it is unlikely that he would willingly have subjected Lucrezia to that particular injury. Once achieved, it was finished, the matter hushed up and Lucrezia banished, with her tears and protests, to Nepi. But it marked a moment of significant change in the relative statures of father and son. 'The pope loves—and has great fear of—his son the duke.'

At the end of September Cesare left to continue the conquest of Romagna, pausing to visit his sister at Nepi *en route*. There was a curiously close relationship between the two—she seems, indeed, to have been the only human being with whom he established any real contact, the only person who could penetrate the façade of mechanical charm with which he faced the world. Again and again during his whirlwind campaigns he would suddenly descend upon her, riding perhaps scores of miles in order to spend an hour or two with her. His affection did not prevent his resenting the favours that her father showered upon her, but that resentment sprang from the knowledge that the immense revenues granted her were necessarily diverted from him—and he needed money for his vast schemes. On her side, Lucrezia was his most loyal ally and constant admirer. When later, as Duchess of Ferrara, she bore a still-born child and collapsed both mentally and physically, it was Cesare alone who could rally her. The doctors reported that they had attempted to bleed her, but she had stubbornly refused. Cesare arrived suddenly at the palace, and persuaded her to allow the operation. 'We bled Madam on the right foot. It was exceedingly difficult to accomplish, and we could not have done it but for the Duke who held her foot—he made her laugh and cheered her greatly.'

The murder of Alfonso had obviously threatened their relationship, and Cesare's visit was probably designed to put his side of the case. There had been well-founded rumours that the Duke of Bisceglie had intended an attack on Cesare—if only to forstall the inevitable attack on him—and Borgia apologists skilfully used the rumours as justification. However Cesare argued the matter, he succeeded. A few weeks later Lucrezia returned to Rome and happily resumed her old life, the tragedy forgotten and the breach in the Borgia family healed.

From Nepi, Cesare marched on to Pesaro where Lucrezia's ex-husband Giovanni Sforza waited in growing fear. Sforza had made desperate appeals to his neighbours for aid but, apart from a token contingent of men sent from Mantua, he was ignored. Before Cesare left Rome he had taken the precaution of sounding the Venetians on their attitude to Sforza and the Serenissima had discreetly let it be known that their protection would be withdrawn. Sforza's anguished debate as to whether he would fight or not was swiftly solved for him. The citizens grasped the opportunity to rid themselves of the irritations of a petty tyrant, rebelled, and he barely escaped with his life. Long before the vanguard of Cesare's army was in sight of Pesaro, the city was added to his growing empire. His entry was another triumph, representatives of the civil government escorting him to the palace in which his sister had ruled four years earlier. There he was accorded, freely and with the consent of the people, the title of Lord of Pesaro.

View of Venice c. 1480, by Breydenbach (Mansell Collection)

4. The Duke of Romagna

The Castle at Ferrara (Italian State Tourist Office)

Among the thousands of people who watched the entry of Cesare Borgia into Pesaro on 27 October was a certain Pandolfo Collenuccio, scholar, poet and diplomat of considerable experience. He had once been a counsellor of Giovanni Sforza—Sforza, indeed, had owed much of his success to Collenuccio's skill—but Collenuccio, falling victim to the usual caprice of the small tyrant, had been imprisoned and eventually escaped to find refuge in Ferrara. He was now present in Pesaro at the urgent request of his host, the Duke of Ferrara, who was most anxious to know the qualities and motives of the new Lord of Pesaro. There was a long-standing friendship between the house of Este of Ferrara and the Borgia, but that did not reduce the Duke's anxiety at having Cesare Borgia as close neighbour.

Two days after Cesare's entry, Collenuccio wrote to Ferrara. It was a long report and, on the whole, bore encouraging news. But the report did more than convey political information. By now the legend of Cesare Borgia was achieving its epic proportions, each victim in the trail of broken enemies in his wake contributing to it as apologia and revenge. Collenuccio, aware that false information was more dangerous than none, was concerned to correct the legend of the invincible monster and, as a competent diplomat, give his master as accurate an assessment as possible upon which rational policy could be built. His portrait of Cesare, therefore, became a piece of documentary evidence of considerable value.

Collenuccio began by confirming that the citizens of Pesaro had, indeed, freely conferred their city upon Cesare. Not only that, but the small city of Fano some miles distant had also expressed its desire to be included in the growing state. Astonishingly, 'he refused, but the citizens insisted and the place is his when he wants it'. Collenuccio had had bitter experience of the terror and destruction caused even by Italian soldiers in a defeated state, and thought it worthwhile to record that the mixed national troops under Valentino's command were behaving in an exemplary manner. More than 2,000 men were quartered in Pesaro 'but had done no appreciable damage'.

Immediately on Cesare's arrival Collenuccio requested an audience. At 8 p.m. Ramiro de Lorqua, Cesare's Chief of Staff, had called upon him. De Lorqua had a singularly evil reputation but on this evening he bore himself with the politeness of a courtier, asking if Collenuccio were comfortable, saying that he had but to ask for his desires to be granted.

On the following morning a courier arrived bearing gifts and an apology. The gifts were lavish, reflecting that carefully planned generosity which was swelling Cesare's expenses to 1,800 ducats daily. A sack of barley, a cask of wine, a sheep, sixteen capons and hens, two large torches, two bundles of wax candles, two boxes of sweetmeats—more than sufficient for Collenuccio to stage his own banquet if he wished. The courier apologized on behalf of his master because the hour for the audience had not yet been arranged. The Duke was suffering from a sore in the groin—being evidently a victim of that 'French disease' which, the Italians claimed, was one of the legacies of the army of Charles VIII.

Collenuccio had his audience earlier on the day that he was

writing. The veteran diplomat was obviously impressed by the young man's skill in the art of verbal fencing—nevertheless he was convinced that Cesare's protestations of friendship for Ferrara were sincere. Collenuccio saw nothing of the blood-maddened demon of popular mythology: the picture he presented to his master was of a cool-headed politician, no more anxious to begin an unnecessary war than any other sensible general in a newly-established base.

The diplomat passed on one additional titbit of gossip gained, not from Cesare, but a Portuguese soldier in his command. The Pope, it was said, was contemplating giving Pesaro to Lucrezia and had found an Italian husband for her, who would be a good friend of Cesare's: 'Whether this be true I know not, but it is generally believed'.

And finally, Collenuccio presented a thumbnail sketch of Cesare's working habits.

> He goes to bed between three and five o'clock in the morning. Consequently, his dawn occurs at one o'clock in the afternoon: 2 p.m. is his sunrise and he gets up at 3 p.m. Immediately on arising, he sits down to breakfast, and while there attends to business affairs. He is considered brave, strong and generous and it is said he sets great store by straightforward men. He is terrible in revenge—so many tell me. In my opinion he is a man of strong good sense, thirsting for greatness and fame: he seems more eager to seize states than to keep and administer them.

Collenuccio was inaccurate in his last judgement. A constant factor in Cesare's Romagna campaign was the ease with which he captured city after city. In only one case was resistance prolonged and that was at Faenza whose young lord was genuinely loved by his people. It was no coincidence that those cities which yielded the easiest were those with the most despotic lords. The Romagnols had long suffered under a series of despicable tyrants, little men who maintained their precarious hold only through alliances with the outside world. The all-embracing policy of Alexander had dissolved the strength of the alliances, leaving individual rulers to face his son alone. Their people had no heart, because they had no motive, for resistance: as often as not they rebelled outright, welcoming the advent of the greater power represented by Valentino.

They were not disillusioned. Cesare imposed good government upon the captured cities: a fact which even his bitterest enemies were forced to acknowledge. They might claim, with justice, that it was only a means to an end: that if it suited his tactics Cesare would as willingly obliterate a city as reform its corrupt government. But for the inarticulate mass of the people, the mass who remained largely indifferent as to the device on the banner which happened to float over the fortress, the Borgia rule was the best they had known for over 150 years—ever since the great legate Cardinal Albornoz had restored order in the Papal States on behalf of a Papacy in self-imposed exile in Avignon.

Under Cesare's rule roads and bridges were repaired and, above all, policed. The bandits who had infested the area, taking advantage of the fragmentation of power, were ruthlessly exterminated. Within the cities price regulations came into operation, controlling the cost of living. Justice was again available to all. It still remained within the framework of the prince's interest but that interest was no longer petty, prepared to starve a province to furnish a mistress's bed-chamber. Again, Cesare was fortunate in the enormous power that backed him. Amply supplied with funds drawn from the Church itself he could afford to be generous and not only refrain from increasing the burden of his new subjects, but in certain cases, actually reduce taxation.

It was this aspect of Valentino's career that attracted the attention of the Florentine secretary of state, Niccolo Machiavelli, and, for a time, persuaded him that here was the Messiah come to save Italy from itself. The Romagna could not have been better designed as a working model to demonstrate the evils that afflicted Italy ever since the fall of the Roman Empire. Here was shown, in miniature, the results of the continual fragmentation of power: minor lordlings with high titles uneasily tyrannizing minute states, conspiring with and against each other solely to maintain their sterile power. And in the chaos thus created, foreign nations could invade and work their will unchecked. 'If Italy must be under the sway of a despot, let it be an Italian despot' was the burden of Machiavelli's argument—and of many others. The aggrandizement of the Borgia did not seem, in that context, too high a price to pay.

Two more cities had fallen painlessly to Cesare before he tackled the toughest problem he had so far encountered, the siege of Faenza. In Rimini, the degenerate descendant of the great Malatesta thought it prudent to sell out rather than test the loyalty of his subjects and escaped into obscurity with the tattered remnants of his honour transmuted into gold. The little city of Cesena had made over-tures even before Cesare's campaign began and now welcomed him. Cesena with its central position in the Romagna, was a useful acquisition and Cesare thereafter used it as his base of operations. He then turned upon Faenza.

Astorre Manfredi, by Leonardo Scaletti (Mansell Collection)

During his conversation with Collenuccio Cesare had remarked: 'I don't know what Faenza wants to do. She can give us no more trouble than did the others. Still, she may delay matters.' Collenuccio had made the discreet reply that greater resistance conferred greater honour on the victor—he knew, as well as did Cesare that the capture of Faenza would entail rather more than a brave show of arms. The city was virtually a republic. True, there was a lord, young Astorre Manfredi who was genuinely popular with the people. But he was only sixteen and, with a sound commonsense that few young despots showed, he still allowed himself to be guided by the Council that had run the city ever since his accession at the age of six. Faenza therefore, though outwardly a despotism with the advantages arising from a despot's dynastic connections, also enjoyed a considerable range of self-government.

Cesare's army arrived under the walls of Faenza on 10 November. It speaks much for his supreme confidence in his military ability that twice he began a major campaign at the beginning of the traddditional close season of winter. The second time he was unfortunate. The winter of 1500 was far worse even than that of the previous year, when his army had had the protection of the city of Forli while it besieged Caterina's castle. Torrential rain succeeded gales: snow came early and by December the land was in the grip of hard frost. And stubbornly Faenza continued to resist. A well-supplied walled city with a garrison in good heart could still wear down a besieging force, even though it were supplied with artillery.

Cesare was forced to strike camp before the end of November: with supplies dwindling and his army exposed to the savage weather there was little else that he could do. He retired with the bulk of his army to Cesena, but his firm control over much of the Romagna made it possible for him to mount a rigorous blockade of Faenza. The roads leading to the city were continually policed, cutting off all supplies. Detachments of rested men took it in turns to maintain pressure on the city itself, so that throughout the winter the citizens were under continual apprehension that a major attack was about to be made.

In March, the main body of the army again took up the actual siege. Faenza had now been cut off from the outside world for five months. Supplies were running dangerously low, the people were wearied and must have known that there was only one end but, incredibly, they rallied. The story of its last days became a minor epic, the details repeated again and again by writers who had long been accustomed to accept civic treachery as the norm. The rich supplied the poor from their own private stocks of food, lent money interest free to Astorre to pay the troops. The priests consented to the despoiling of the very altars, equably watching the sacred vessels melted down to provide bullion for the financing of the war against the son of their spiritual overlord. The women themselves took active part in the defence. Cesare was impressed, declaring that with such troops behind him he could conquer all Italy. He gave force to his admiration by hanging a certain Bernardo Grammante, a dyer of the town who escaped and sought to betray it by pointing out a weak section of the defences. Grammante was executed for treachery—but the siege guns were immediately moved up to batter the indicated spot.

They made a breach at last and, after ferocious hand-to-hand fighting, the Council informed their lord that further resistance was useless. Astorre agreed, envoys were sent to Cesare, and the fighting ceased. According to his habitual policy in the Romagna, Cesare gave the city good terms. 'Indulgence for the small people, rigorous control of the great,' was followed in Faenza as elsewhere.

Astorre Manfredi and his illegitimate half-brother were handed over to Cesare. They cherished, perhaps, optimistic views on their future. Cesare treated them with the respect due to their rank, carried them around for him for a while and then packed them off to Rome. They found their way into the great castle of Sant Angelo, at about the time that Caterina Sforza was leaving it, and disappeared thereafter from the sight of the curious. The next that the world knew about them was recorded in Burchard's diary: their bodies had been found floating in the Tiber.

'In order to preserve a newly acquired State particular attention should be given to two objectives. In the first place, care should be taken entirely to extinguish the family of the ancient sovereigns: in the second, laws should not be changed nor taxes increased.' In Machiavelli's opinion Cesare, in the person of the Prince, acted prudently in murdering the Manfredi children. Further on in that slight, enigmatic treatise which was to make his name a synonym for all evil, Machiavelli hammered the point home. Discussing 'whether fortresses are really of service to a prince' he used the case of Caterina Sforza to prove that they were of little value. Fortresses always fell if the attack was determined enough. 'When she was attacked by Cesare Borgia, she must doubtless then, though perhaps too late, have become convinced that the best fortress for a prince is found in the people's affection.' Caterina was ultimately freed, on pressure from the French, because the Borgia had nothing more to fear from

Ludovico Il Moro, by Maestro della Pala Sforzesca (Photo Scala, Florence)

Sixtus IV and his court, by Melozzo da Forli (Photo Scala, Florence)

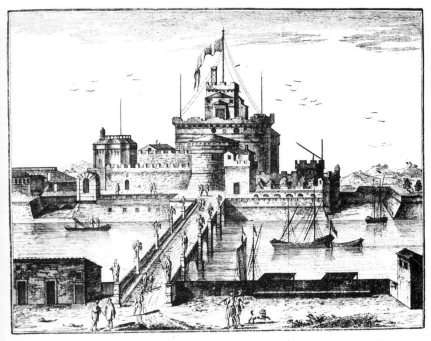

her. Her craven sons had signed away their inheritance in exchange for gold or contemptuously bestowed ecclesiastic preferment. The Forlivese had not the slightest intention of rising on behalf of their hated mistress and Caterina could therefore be allowed to end her days in a convent. Similarly, Cesare had nothing to fear from the majority of the dispossessed rulers. Astorre Manfredi, however, was genuinely beloved of his people who would undoubtedly have risen had there been any hope of affecting a restoration. The better the prince, the more certain his death.

Cesare's moves after the fall of Faenza were swift and widespread. First he marched on Bologna, but then was forced to swing away after an unequivocal warning that the city was under the protection of France. Then he turned south, deliberately, almost provocatively entering the hitherto sacrosanct territory of Florence. The Florentine Signoria were faced with three choices: fight, appeal to Louis, or buy Cesare off. They appealed to Louis but meanwhile Cesare's army marched to within six miles of the walls of Florence. The sight of an inimical army so close had not been seen in Florence for over a generation and they hastily compounded with Cesare. Officially, he was to enter their pay as a *condottiero* at a salary of 36,000 ducats a year. Both sides knew that it was but a paper transaction, that the arms of Cesare Borgia would be wielded only for Cesare Borgia—but only one side knew that no payment would ever be made.

Cesare continued his march through Tuscany, crossing the peninsula at high speed to the Tyrrhenian coast, there to lay siege to the city of Piombino. It was a dramatic change in his policy which, hitherto, had been concentrated on the eastern coast. The capture of Piombino would give him a base whence attack could be launched into the Florentine heartlands, eventually drawing a ring of steel around the Republic. So the Signoria observed with something near despair. But Cesare still was aware of the protecting power of France behind Florence and so moved cautiously. And while Piombino was still holding out, his father recalled him to Rome for great events were on the move.

Throughout, Louis of France had looked upon Naples as his ultimate goal. The capture of Milan, the unleashing of the Borgia hydra—these were mere steps to that end. But his courage failed him at the last: over the past centuries army after army had been engulfed in the quicksands of Neapolitan politics and those which survived fell swift victim to the treacherous climate of the south which even the Italians of the north had feared. Doubtful of his ability to triumph where so many others had failed, he thought of a compromise—sharing both the difficulties and the rewards with the King of Spain. It was, in Machiavelli's expert opinion, the biggest single mistake of his career and one from which all the long misery of Italy flowed. 'If the king of France was powerful enough to invade the kingdom of Naples, he ought to have done it: but if he was not able, he should not have divided it.'

But Louis totally lacked Machiavelli's perception. The Aragonese dynasty which ruled Naples was closely related to the royal house of Spain but, smoothly, Ferdinand of Spain agreed to betray his relative, Frederic of Naples: smoothly he agreed that the spoils were to be equally divided between himself and Louis with the pope allowed to pick up the scraps. For one other formality was needed—a papal bull to dispossess the Christian king of Naples in order that his territories could be divided between the Christian kings of France and Spain. Alexander agreed readily. There was some difficulty in finding pretext for the bull. Frederic was a very good king, the best that Naples had had for a long and dismal period and his personal morals were irreproachable. But he was foolish enough to be on good terms with the Turks—a reasonable policy considering the trade needs of his kingdom, but a fatal one now. Eight years before Alexander himself had made desperate attempts to make an alliance with the Sultan to stem the first French invasion. Now, on behalf of the French king, he declared Frederic deposed on the grounds that he was a traitor to Christendom and so blessed the coming rape of Naples as a crusade.

Alexander had good personal reasons. His son Cesare still needed Louis's support. But in addition to this constant policy was the fact that in the south of Italy were the rich lands of the Colonna and Savelli families—lands which could be used to endow Lucrezia's son and his own little son by Giulia Farnese. As a bonus, unimportant but not less sweet, was the avenging of that three-year-old insult offered to the Borgia when Frederic's daughter Carlotta had contemptuously rejected Cesare.

Cesare arrived in Rome on June 13, 1501, having left a large detachment of his troops still besieging Piombino. His titles now were resounding for, after the fall of Faenza, Alexander had granted him the style of Duke of Romagna in reasonable anticipation of later conquests, and he could call himself, 'Cesare Borgia of France, Duke of Valentinois, Duke of Romagna, Captain General, Gonfaloniere of the Roman Church', supreme head of the armed Church, entitled to bear among his many banners the great white Gonfalon with the device of the golden keys. The French army arrived six days later and camped outside Rome. Burchard made his customary meticulous notes, recording without comment the fact that the wretched residents who had already paid to avoid having soldiers billeted on them were nevertheless forced to take them. He also noted the provisions sent out to the officers of the holy army by the papal commissioners: '150 casks of wine, bread, meat, eggs, cheese, fruit and other necessities, including sixteen specially chosen prostitutes for those particular needs'.

The actual campaign was an anti-climax. Treachery hastened the end of the ruling house of Naples, as it had marked the beginning. Frederic had confided two major fortresses into the care of the great Spanish general Gonsalvo, a man who had served his family well, and Gonsalvo yielded them. But the speed of the collapse did not prevent that almost ritual blood sacrifice of Italians which marked every foreign invasion. On this occasion the victim was the city of Capua and the leaders of the sacrificers were themselves Italian.

Frederic had retreated to the city and the people defended him loyally. Even after five days of continual bombardment the defence remained strong—but the inevitable traitor appeared and, on 25 July, Cesare's troops gained entry though a treacherously opened gate. Afterwards, no one could give any rational explanation of the

Castel Nuovo, the Maschi Angioino, Naples (J. Allan Cash)

carnage that followed. Centuries of warfare between roughly equal cities had taught the Italians that massacre of a defeated enemy was a two-edged weapon, certain to turn upon the temporary victors. For over a hundred years now, inter-city wars had been fought by mercenaries and the defeated paid in gold, not blood. The massacre of Capua was probably due in part to the fact that foreign troops formed the bulk of Cesare's army, but the native Italians joined in with equal ferocity. Women, as usual, suffered the most with inevitable rape preceding murder. Thirty of the most beautiful were captured and sent to Rome, Christians sent to the seat of Christendom as though to the court of a pagan prince. It was a Frenchman who recorded this incident, leaving it to Italian writers to elaborate it into a Herculean myth whereby Cesare took the women into his personal harem.

In Rome, the successes of the holy crusade were credited almost entirely to Cesare. Burchard heard of the sack of Capua on the following day and that, too, found a place in his diary, written with the same passion that he recorded details of etiquette and provisioning.

On the night of 26 July the Pope heard of Don Cesare's capture of Capua...a triumph which crowned the events of the past ten days. A

49

citizen of Capua—a certain Fabrizio—admitted Don Cesare's soldiers by treachery. They killed him, however, and afterwards they killed about 3,000 ordinary soldiers and 200 knights and many citizens and priests as well as monks and nuns in churches and convents. The women were treated most cruelly, and the girls were raped or seized as booty. It is estimated that about 6,000 people were killed.

Later, Alexander made a tour of the territories that were now part of the Borgia empire, greeted by papal soldiers firing off arms and crying, with well-rehearsed enthusiasm, 'Borgia! Borgia!'

But the Neapolitan campaign was merely a side-show for Cesare. He had placed Louis of France in his debt, more revenue was directed into the Borgia coffers—but it was in central Italy that his interests lay. Northern and southern Italy were frontier states, their possession eternally disputed by giants: only in the centre was there relative freedom to pursue that goal which was now being slowly revealed—the acquisition of a base on which he could erect not merely a dukedom but a kingdom.

The southern approach to his state in the Romagna was now secure. The possessions of three great Roman families—Colonna, Savelli and Gaetani—had once menaced this approach but after the destruction of their Neapolitan ally, Alexander was able to confiscate the territories wholesale and distribute them in his immediate family. The northern approach to the Romagna was still comparatively vulnerable: there was only the duchy of Ferrara between Cesare and French-held Milan on one side and Venice on the other. An attack on Ferrara was unthinkable for it would immediately arouse the resentment of his great ally France and, far worse, the enmity of Venice: nobody wanted an ambitious Cesare as immediate neighbour.

Bribery was the only alternative to attack, and the Borgia family possessed in Lucrezia a bribe of remarkable potency. Even during the lifetime of her second husband, there had been talk of marrying her into the Este family and three months after his death the complicated negotiations had begun with Alfonso, the son of the widowed Duke Ercole, as potential bridegroom. The negotiations met with considerable difficulty. King Louis of France wanted the young man as husband for a French princess—but at the same time he desperately needed Alexander's support in the Neapolitan affair for only Alexander could invest him with the conquered state. At length, deciding in favour of a Neapolitan crown, he withdrew his objections and now actually urged the Duke to accept the Borgia proposals.

Ercole disliked the whole matter but, under continual French pressure—and threatened with the prospect of being deposed as a disobedient son of the Church—he gave way. He demanded a stiff price and got it: a dowry of 200,000 ducats, a heavy reduction in the dues that he paid to the Church and other, lesser, concessions which would strengthen his autonomy. There remained only the question of gaining the consent of his son Alfonso, the bridegroom elect.

Alfonso objected, strongly. He may, or may not, have had grounds to suspect that the bride's moral character was sullied beyond redemption. The tales of incest, of promiscuity, of an illegitimate child were possibly the inventions of enemies and were certainly irrelevant. Virtue was not the prime consideration in a dynastic bride. But he had excellent grounds to object on the score of personal well-being. Two Spanish noblemen who had believed themselves all but married to this particular bride had found themselves dismissed like stableboys. Her first husband had been divorced to the accompaniment of mocking laughter: her second had been murdered, almost certainly by her brother. But so urgent was Ercole's desire to bring about a marriage between his house and that of Borgia that he threatened, if necessary, to marry the girl himself. Alfonso gave way—and found, in fact, that he had acquired an unusually good wife: gay, cultured, faithful and, ultimately, loving. Lucrezia was ever adaptable.

With her marriage, Cesare felt himself secure in his base. The house of Este was linked by blood and marriage to the lordly houses of Mantua in the north and Urbino in the south. His new Dukedom of Romagna was protected by a double ring of steel and matrimonial alliances, secure from outside enemies. But the threat that nearly unseated him shortly after Lucrezia's marriage came from within.

5. The Prince

Il Condottiere, by Da Vinci (Mansell Collection)

The court that had grown up around Cesare was composed of three distinct groups of people.

At the very heart, forming a kind of steel core, were the men who had identified themselves with him at the beginning of his career. They were soldiers, not politicians, and most of them were Spaniards. Apart from the strong tie of race, Cesare could count to a high degree upon their support because they were aliens among a people who feared and hated Spaniards. Three of them achieved a species of immortality, the pale reflection of their master's: Michelotto, Sebastiano Pinzone and Ramiro de Lorqua. Lorqua, noted for his cruelty even in that band of cruel men, was made Governor of the

Romagna, his powers second only to Cesare's. Michelotto was the duke's right-hand man, his friend—insofar as any man could claim friendship with the cold young man—his general and his executioner. Most murders by obvious violence were those of his staging. Sebastiano Pinzone, a more shadowy figure, was commonly referred to as the duke's poisoner—an appellation arising more probably from his secretive methods than from any particular skill he may have had with poison.

On the fringe of this inner core was the usual colourful, evanescent court of poets and artists, diplomats, writers and professional courtiers who would be attracted to any rising man. Cesare shared the usual Renaissance pretensions to universal culture. At Cesena he was building up a superb library, largely furnished by robbery. He patronized sculptors and painters—a mandatory patronage for any prince who desired to pass as civilized but one which he exercised with some discernment. Scholars gravitated to his court—not very many and not very great scholars if for no better reason than that the restless, peripatetic nature of the court was hardly conducive to learning. Cesare himself seems to have had small interest in the current passionate interest in the classics. Despite his ecclesiastic training he had little knowledge of Latin. Italian he spoke when he had to: Spanish was his preferred tongue among intimates.

But if scholars received little encouragement from him, architects and engineers were certain of lucrative employment. Bridges, roads, water-supplies, forts—these were the nerves and sinews of his State and their maintenance was all important. It was as engineer pure and simple that Leonardo da Vinci entered his service some time after the year 1500. After the fall of Milan and the destruction of Leonardo's current patron Lodovico Sforza, the artist had sought another purchaser for his more marketable talents and found ready employment with Cesare. His major tasks were the repair of the siege-battered fortresses in the Romagna and the establishment of fortifications for the siege of Piombino.

And finally there was the third group—the *condottieri*—territorial lords who had placed their swords at the disposal of the duke, wolves temporally harnessed by a greater wolf: the men who fought his wars.

Apart from a doubtful incident at Capua when he was reported to have led the cavalry charge that broke the Colonna, there was only one recorded instance of Cesare actually fighting on a battlefield—and that was the skirmish in which he was killed. His major military talent lay in his ability to move with incredible speed, to appear before the walls of a town when his victims believed he was miles away. But even this was merely the necessary adjunct to a political talent—the ability to deceive the victim as to his intentions.

Every man who knew him—and they included such as Machiavelli and the Venetian ambassadors, men trained to the last degree in the art of character assessment—agreed that his ability to disguise his thoughts and control his emotions amounted to the inhuman. It was impossible to know whether he was in a towering rage or gloating with satisfaction: he appeared exactly the same whether he was on the brink of triumph or facing total disaster. In this he differed radically from his father who reacted impulsively, extravagantly, to the changes of fortune, crying or laughing or raging as the occasion demanded. Cesare listened, said nothing, and acted.

'He turned the art of war into the art of deceit—and thereafter all others copied him' was the judgement of a Perugian diplomat. Cesare had little knowledge of, because he had little use for, conventional warfare. He possessed the one ability vital for a military commander—that of controlling men in the mass. Behind the easily assumed charm was a genuinely terrifying personality which seemed to exert an almost hypnotic influence, capable of quelling the most ruffianly freebooter. On one occasion a group of his men panicked while crossing a river. The officers tried in vain to restore order: the chaos grew worse, with the danger that hundreds of men might drown. It stopped, abruptly, when the duke rode his horse to the river-bank and sat, totally silent, looking on. Normally, after the capture of a city there would ensue two or three days of total disorder while the victorious army plundered and murdered—it was the men's expected right and any attempt to deprive them of it would usually lead to immediate mutiny. In the cities that Cesare captured, order prevailed within hours of the surrender—if it so suited him.

But though his military talents were perfectly adequate for the civic dominance which was his objective, he was hampered by lack of men. True, he had the troops loaned to him by Louis but they possessed that weakness of all auxiliaries which Machiavelli noted. 'When defeated, the Prince suffers the consequences: when victorious he lies at the mercy of such armies'. At the beginning of his career Cesare had no territorial troops of his own: he therefore had to employ those of other Italian princes—and the princes themselves.

The *condottieri* had risen some two hundred years earlier when the cities of Italy, grown wealthy and soft, had preferred to pay mercenaries to fight their endless wars rather than watch the decimation of their own citizens. Initially, the mercenaries had all been foreigners but swiftly the trade passed into the hands of native Italians. A local lordling, gathering together a few hundred retainers, would march out and offer his sword to the highest bidder. The chances of his being killed in battle were little higher than of being murdered in a street brawl, for mercenary wars were fought on clearcut lines. The rewards were potentially immense. The great Sforza dynasty of Milan had been founded by a *condottiero* who had turned his sword against his employers: the Malatesta of Rimini and the Montefeltre of Urbino had established their dazzling courts on the proceeds of such legal banditry.

There was therefore an ample pool of men upon whom Cesare could draw. The difficulty lay in controlling, not the men themselves, but their leaders, each of whom saw himself as an independent power and was possessed of but one objective—his personal aggrandizement. One of Cesare's *condottieri*—Vitellozo Vitelli—had an additional and, in Italian eyes, honourable motive for casting in his lot with Cesare's—revenge. Vitelli's brother had been in the employ of Florence and the Florentines had, quite properly, executed him for treachery. Thereafter, Vitelli's prime consideration was the destruction of Florence—a desire which was to cause Cesare great danger.

But the other *condottieri* were cast in the ordinary mould. Among them were members of the great Roman family of the Orsini—Paolo and Francesco Orsini, the latter being a duke in his own right. Pope Alexander had skilfully used the mortal hatred that the Orsini family held for their hereditary enemies, the Colonna, to break the hold of the Colonna in Rome and the Orsini looked now upon themselves as special allies of the Borgia.

Typical of Cesare's *condottieri* was that Oliverotto da Fermo whose career Machiavelli chose to illustrate his thesis that a man could achieve sovereignty through crime. Oliverotto had been brought up by his uncle, the lord of Fermo, who had treated him as a beloved son. The young man went off to make his fortune as a *condottiero* and, in due course, intimated to his uncle that he desired to visit his childhood home. The uncle prepared a magnificent reception to welcome and honour the young man, who repaid it by massacring the uncle and his entire family during the banquet and established himself as lord of Fermo. He was still firmly established when the lure of banditry seized him again, and he offered his sword to Cesare.

It was inevitable that conflict should arise between these men and their temporary overlord, and the seeds of dissension were sown while Cesare was absent on the Neapolitan campaign. The *condottiero* efficiently discharged his immediate orders—the capture of Piombino, but almost immediately afterwards, Vitelozzo Vitelli went off on a freelance operation on his own. Still cherishing his deep hatred for Florence, he crossed over into the Florentine state and successfully produced a rebellion in the subject city of Arezzo. The Aretines gained nothing from it for they merely exchanged the civilized rule of Florence for that of Vitelli and his fellow ruffian, Giovanni Baglioni.

Florence immediately protested to Louis that Cesare was violating her territory—a reasonable protest, for a *condottiero* was assumed to be acting under the orders of his principal. On the previous occasion when Cesare had threatened Florentine safety Louis's reaction had been unequivocal. 'We have twice told our captains in Italy that if Valentino should threaten either Florence or Bologna they were to attack him without further warning.' The promise was fulfilled, and French troops began to march towards Arezzo.

Cesare was meanwhile back in the Romagna. The news from Tuscany caused him some perplexity. In principle, he had no objection whatsoever to the harrying of Florence: sooner or later a clash between himself and the great republic was inevitable. But that must come only when he was prepared for it. His *condottieri* were threatening his vital relationship with France—but on the other hand he had no intention of going to war with them in order to protect Florence. In the situation he temporized, sending an urgent message to Florence with the request that they should despatch an envoy with whom he could discuss the matter.

The Florentine Signoria were still suspiciously debating the matter, when the object of their suspicions executed the neatest piece of treachery that even he had yet executed, gaining thereby the entire Duchy of Urbino with scarcely the loss of a man.

Guidobaldo Montefeltro, the Duke of Urbino, had good reasons to suppose himself secure in his home. He was not merely a paper ally of the Borgias but, when Cesare himself was merely a seventeen-year-old cardinal, Montefeltro had been in command of the papal forces, fighting to establish Alexander's position in the precarious first months of his pontificate. Later, Guidobaldo found himself part of the Borgia matrimonial network, for his wife was a relative of the Ferrara dynasty into which Lucrezia had married. Cesare, throughout his Romagna campaign, had been careful to treat Guidobaldo with the greatest respect and, later, with

Ducal Palace, Urbino (Italian State Tourist Office)

that familiar affection due to relatives by even distant marriage. When, therefore, Guidobaldo received requests for supplies and troops to reinforce Cesare's, he was ready to oblige. Cesare told him that he was marching to attack Camerino and asked for 1,000 men. They formed a very substantial part of Urbino's defences but Guidobaldo, anxious to maintain his good relations with the Borgia, sent them off. If he had any doubts, he quieted them with the knowledge that Cesare was a long way off and that, if danger threatened, there would be ample time to call out the militia.

Guidobaldo was at supper three days later when news was brought that Cesare, moving with immense speed, had entered the Duchy in the south. Simultaneously, two other groups were advancing from the north and east: a total of some 6,000 men were converging upon Urbino itself—an Urbino that was denuded of troops.

Guidobaldo had no other choice but to run. He was a brave man but he was also that rarity, a good Romagnol prince: his people would fight for him, but there was little point in subjecting them to all the horrors of street warfare merely to delay the inevitable by two or three days. He escaped, making his way with considerable difficulty through a countryside swarming with enemy soldiers, and ultimately reached the protection of his brother-in-law's court at Mantua. From there, he wrote a pathetic letter to Cardinal Giuliano della Rovere, begging him to inform King Louis of the incredible treachery. 'I cannot understand why I have been so treated, for I have always sought to please both the Pope and Duke Valentino. Indeed, two Spanish noblemen came to me from His Holiness, bearing a letter in which His Holiness assured me that always he had held me to be a good son of the Holy See, and therefore asked me to aid the Duke in his enterprises.' Guidobaldo was particularly indignant at the rumour that his own people had rebelled. 'They say that Valentino claims that my people drove me out. I swear—they wept when they heard of my flight.'

A few hours after Guidobaldo had fled from Urbino, Cesare was installed in his palace—that beautiful palace of the Montefeltri which had been a cradle for the infant culture of the Renaissance. And it was there that the Florentine embassy waited upon him at two o'clock on the morning of 25 June 1502.

The leader of the embassy was an ecclesiastic, Francesco Soderini, Bishop of Volterra. His secretary was a pale young bureaucrat of thirty-three, Niccolo Machiavelli, now meeting for the first time the man whose name had predominated in so many anxious debates of

Courtyard of ducal palace, Urbino (Photo Scala, Florence)

the Signoria. Soderini did the talking, but it was from the secretary's letters that the Florentine Signoria gained an insight into the character and possible motives of their opponent. Machiavelli wrote in his first, necessarily hurried, assessments:

> 'This duke is a man of splendour and magnificence. He has great confidence in himself, treating the greatest enterprise as though it were a small thing. In his search for glory and the increasing of his dominions he will deny himself rest, treating fatigue and peril alike with contempt. Before it is even known that he has left one place, he has settled himself in another. His soldiers love him, and he has chosen the best in Italy. Good fortune follows him. Altogether, he is a successful man—and one to be feared.'

The first embassy ended inconclusively, as Cesare intended. He

View in the Romagna, by Poussin (National Gallery)

St Catherine disputing, by Pintoricchio, in the Borgia Apartments, Vatican (Photo Scala, Florence)

Niccolo Machiavelli, by Santi di Tito (Mansell Collection)

had opened it with a sweeping, almost petulant, attack on the Florentine Signoria itself: he did not approve of it and if the Florentines really wished for his friendship they would have to change their method of government. The attack invited, and received, the retort that the Florentines had no intention of meddling with their constitution in order to please Duke Valentino. Soderini then swung over to the direct attack himself. If Valentino was really anxious for Florentine friendship he would order Vitelli to surrender Arezzo. Cesare riposted with a skilful two-pronged return. He had no control over Vitelli, who was carrying out a private vendetta—with King Louis's consent and encouragement.

The reply halted Soderini in his tracks. Louis might, indeed, be engaged in double-dealing: the whole pattern of Florentine alliances might have changed within the past few days—or hours. It was well known that Cesare had means of gaining swift and accurate information denied to others. The Duke pressed home his advantage—knowing that it might very well be possible to wring concessions from Florence during this period of doubt. He gave the Signoria exactly four days to decide whether they would have him for friend or enemy, and gave Machiavelli leave to depart immediately with his message. Soderini remained with him.

Louis of France had his own problems. The neat carving up of the Neapolitan State between himself and Spain had not gone according to plan. Spain was demanding more and more—precisely as Machiavelli had foreseen—and full scale war between the French and Spanish armies in southern Italy was only a matter of time—and very little time at that. And now he was apparently to be forced to choose between Florence and Cesare Borgia, between the wealthy Tuscan bankers and the descendant of a Spanish house who might suddenly remember the ties of blood and throw in his lot with Spain. In the situation he, too, temporized. The army group *en route* for Arezzo continued its march and hurled itself upon Vitellozzo Vitelli's company, thus demonstrating that France was honouring its promise. But at the same time, French ambassadors hastened to Florence and to Cesare urging each to give concessions to the other. The King himself was coming into Italy at the head of a great army when he would, in person, smooth out the differences between his ill-assorted allies.

Cesare felt that he had pushed his defiance of France about as far as it was safe to push it and accordingly he ordered Vitelli to agree to an immediate armistice, and withdraw from Tuscany. He backed up the order with the threat that, if Vitelli did not immediately comply, his own city of Città di Castello would be put to the sack. Vitelli obeyed, reluctantly and with furious anger, his attitude an ominous and adequate index to the state of mind of his fellow *condottieri*.

6. The Revolt of the Condottieri

Making cannons, by Poccetti (Photo Scala, Florence)

Louis of France entered Italy in July 1502, committed to that battle with the power of Spain that introduced a generation of misery for Italians. Thirty years later Spain would emerge triumphant, standing erect in the shattered land that had been the battleground for the two super-states.

Left to himself, Louis would probably have devoted his limited talents to his own country rather than dissipate them in yet another ill-starred Italian expedition. An easy-going, self-indulgent man, his steps were guided on to the disastrous path by his highly capable minister, that Georges d'Amboise to whom Cesare had brought a cardinal's hat four years earlier. d'Amboise aimed at nothing less than the papal tiara—an ornament which seemed now to be in the gift of the Borgia family—and he proved to be Cesare's most valuable friend at the royal court of France.

Immediately upon Louis's arrival in Italy, the victims and enemies of Cesare hastened to him to lay their interminable, and justified, complaints and protests before the only man who could exert some influence. The numbers of complaints grew steadily, accurately reflecting Cesare's expanding power in central Italy. The Varano family—late lords of Camerino—were the latest victims, bearing the tale of yet another Romagnol city falling to the Borgia onslaught. Its head, old Julius Caesar Varano, had achieved power in the normal Romagnol fashion—his particular crime had been fratricide—but now that he was a dishonoured corpse and his sons the helpless prisoners of the Duke of Romagna, his crimes were forgotten and his blood turned into good propaganda. The Malatesta had been driven out of Rimini where the banner of the Bull now flew. In Bologna the Bentivogli family were looking over their shoulder and making prudent overtures to the enraged Vitellozzo Vitelli. Even the Orsini admitted to unease: clearly, their usefulness to Alexander was over and their territories ripe for harvesting. Rumours abounded, fed by the hopes of frightened men: Louis had come to Italy specially to chastise his insolent protégé: he feared the growing might of Cesare: Cesare would be taken back in chains to France.

In August, Cesare visited Louis in Milan and Louis, far from arresting him, seems to have gone out of his way to make it known that the Duke was his very good friend. In public, before the affronted eyes of those who had hoped to see the Borgia pride laid low, the King of France threw his arms around Cesare's neck, addressing him not merely as an ally but as cousin and most dear kinsman. They spoke for long in private: the details remained secret but the result was soon obvious. Cesare was given a free hand to settle his difficulties in central Italy.

The most pressing of those difficulties was the disaffection rapidly spreading through the *condottieri*: each of them a territorial lord in his own right, each had links with at least one other family who knew themselves to be threatened by the Duke. Information rapidly spread that Louis had withdrawn his protection from Bologna and, so it was said, had actually lent Cesare troops specifically to smash the Orsini. The more urgent motive of fear now replaced the constant motive of ambition and the *condottieri* moved in mutual self-defence.

Cesare was outpaced by events for the first time in his career, the deceiver for once deceived. A few weeks after his return from Milan the *condottieri* revolted in the state of Urbino and arranged for the return of Guidobaldo. As soon as their base was secured they arranged for an impressive conference in which all who had grievances against the Duke could concert their actions. The conference took place in Orsini territory, where victims of Cesare rubbed shoulders with the men who had wrought their destruction in the

Duke's name. Cardinal Orsini presided, with his kinsmen Paolo and Francesco Orsini: Petrucci came from Siena, Baglioni from Bologna, Montefeltre from Urbino. Oliverotto da Fermo, too, was present: he had no immediate grudge against his employer but attended on the sound principle of seeking safety in the majority.

Cesare was at Imola when the news broke. The inner core of his followers remained, as ever, loyal, but the troops at his command were outnumbered by those the *condottieri* could raise. Under the pressure of need he stepped up the recruitment of mercenaries but he increased, too, the recruitment of soldiers from his own dukedom of Romagna. It was a wise move, Machiavelli judged: the native militia were raw recruits compared with veteran mercenaries but they were far more dependable and thereafter Cesare steadily increased the ratio of native to mercenary troops. By October he had some 6,000 men under arms with the promise of more military aid from Louis. But the political threat from Florence was even greater than the immediate military danger from his rebellious *condottieri*. Would the Signoria make common cause with the rebels in order to eradicate the prime source of trouble?

Again he sent to Florence, urgently requesting that an ambassador armed with full powers should be attached to his court. The Signoria were just as anxious to know what was happening in the Romagna but, cannily, they decided to send not an ambassador but an envoy. An ambassador could be manoeuvred into a position where he might make damaging concessions: an envoy without powers preserved all the observational value of an ambassador without the weakness. They sent Niccolò Machiavelli with strict instructions to admit nothing, promise nothing, concede nothing. He was to play Cesare until the situation cleared.

Machiavelli arrived at Imola on 7 October: thereafter, he remained with Cesare almost continually until the end of the year, observing him at close quarters as he felt his way through the perilous, swiftly changing conditions that followed the revolt, and recording the observations with the detachment of an anthropologist. Later, he drew heavily on the experience of these three months to create his enduring portrait of a universal Prince.

Despite his imminent danger, Cesare appeared in an optimistic, almost expansive mood. Even when he learned that the faithful Michelotto had been heavily defeated in the first trial of arms with the rebels, and barely escaped with his life, Cesare appeared undismayed. Doubtless, he was concerned to put a bold face on the matter before Machiavelli, knowing that the Florentine Signoria were being kept closely informed of his reactions. But Machiavelli was convinced that, all evidence to the contrary, Cesare was still in control of events. He warned Machiavelli that the *condottieri* were no friends of the Republic and the Signoria would do well to enter into an alliance with him while they still had the opportunity. 'Secretary, I know who are my friends—and who are my enemies. I am taking you into my confidence. Tell your lords that I wish to count them as friends— if they show themselves as such.'

Machiavelli soon learned the reasons for Cesare's confidence. Inevitably, the *condottieri* had sought to draw Venice into their plans. The Venetians had at first seemed interested, even encouraging, but then, on learning that Cesare still enjoyed the support of Louis, they disentangled themselves. Dismay struck the rebels and immediately the more timorous began to scramble back to solid ground. Still in his remarkably frank mood, Cesare told Machiavelli of the latest moves: 'They have begun to be friends again, writing pretty letters. Paolo [Orsini] is coming today and the Cardinal comes tomorrow. In this way they believe they can trick me. But I tell you, I am merely playing with them. I listen to all they have to say— and take my own time.'

By the end of October the revolt was at an end. The conspirators had found that it needed skill of a very high order to weld into one the conflicting ambitions of a group of independent men, each of whom was aware that his colleagues would betray him at a moment's notice for the sake of immediate gain. Paolo Orsini's mission had been undertaken on behalf of his colleagues, but even he had made it known that he would not be averse to making a separate peace. Cesare accepted the overtures and Machiavelli obediently passed on the details of the peace treaty to Florence. Cesare would renew the engagements of the *condottieri*, on condition that Urbino and Pesaro were returned to him. The *condottieri* cheerfully assented to the abandoning of their wretched tools, Giovanni Sforza and Guido-baldo Montefeltre, whom they had reinstated in their possessions of Pesaro and Urbino. Machiavelli was at first surprised at the ease with which the treaty was signed: it seemed unlikely that such deep and bitter animosity could be patched over. But he later came to the correct conclusion that both parties were merely manoeuvering for a better position—the *condottieri* in order to launch an attack from more solid ground and Cesare with the intention of removing his enemies one by one. An accident, however, enabled him to destroy all of them in one operation—the 'beautiful deception' of Sinigaglia.

On 10 December Cesare left Imola, still accompanied by Machiavelli, marching to the attack on Sinigaglia, a city on the Adriatic coast. The force at the Duke's immediate disposal was impressive, for in addition to the levies and mercenaries was a large contingent of French auxiliaries who were later dismissed. The French were hardly needed, for the *condottieri*, anxious to reinstate themselves in Cesare's good graces, were vigorously assaulting Sinigaglia while he made his leisurely journey across the Romagna. Machiavelli asked discreet questions of all who would answer, and came to the opinion that the dismissal of the French was part of a stratagem to lull the *condottieri* into a feeling of security.

The company halted at Cesena—and immediately Cesare was inundated with complaints against his governor, Ramiro de Lorqua. The Spaniard had ruled energetically in Cesare's name, but simultaneously had indulged in an orgy of cruelty that surpassed even the most depraved of Romagnol tyrants. One of the many tales told against him was of how he had thrust a clumsy page boy into the fire and held him down with a foot while he burned alive.

Cesare was indifferent to the cruelty as such. But de Lorqua's habits had seriously undermined the Borgia control in the areas he governed, for the Romagnols had accepted Cesare's rule only because it delivered them from the arbitrary cruelty of their own lords. There was, too, the matter of a serious deficiency in the supplies which had been sent to Cesena to ward off famine. de Lorqua was summoned from Pesaro to account for his stewardship. The accounting was deemed inadequate: on the morning of 26 December the Cesenese found a carefully arranged tableau in their market place—the headless body of de Lorqua, still clad in its finery, the fierce head itself displayed on a pike and, near it, a bloodstained cutlass.

The body was still in the market place when Cesare left shortly afterwards. At Fano, Vitellozzo Vitelli was waiting for him with the news that Sinigaglia had fallen but that the governor in the citadel had refused to surrender the keys to anyone except Cesare himself. Cesare confirmed that he was marching on to Sinigaglia and requested Vitellozzo and his fellow *condottieri* to remain in Sinigaglia. Almost as an afterthought, he ordered them to remove their troops from the city, giving as reason the fact that his own troops would have to be quartered there.

As soon as Vitellozzo had left, Cesare told eight of his most loyal captains the plan he had in mind. The army was to march to within five miles of Sinigaglia. From there a detachment of 200 lances was to ride forward under the command of Michelotto. Cesare would

follow immediately with the bulk of the force. As soon as they met the four *condottieri*—the two Orsini, Vitellozzo and Oliverotto da Fermo—the eight captains were to move forward and, two to each man, should accompany them back to the city. Care was to be taken not to arouse their suspicions of anything untoward.

The first part of the plan worked smoothly. On the morning of 31 December Vitellozzo and the two Orsini rode out of the city to meet their master, leaving Oliverotto in the main square with about 1,000 men. Machiavelli noticed that 'Vitellozzo—who was wearing only a cloak without any armour underneath—appeared melancholy and dejected, which surprised those who knew his normal courage and bearing'. He was, in fact, suspicious and had tried to talk his colleagues out of the meeting but had been overruled.

Cesare greeted the three men courteously, but noticed immediately that Oliverotto was not present. He made a slight sign to Michelotto who immediately hurried off into the city. Michelotto found Oliverotto and warned him to move his men out of Sinigaglia, otherwise they might come to blows with Cesare's men because of the shortage of quarters. He also pointed out that Cesare would take it amiss if Oliverotto did not come to pay his respects. Oliverotto did as he was advised, dismissed his men and joined his colleagues.

Machiavelli was riding behind and the last he saw of the group was as they disappeared into the palace, still talking amicably, to enjoy the banquet that Cesare had prepared. Piecing together the confused evidence it appeared to him that all the *condottieri*, with the exception of Vitellozzo, were taken utterly by surprise as Cesare's men fell upon them. Vitellozzo managed to kill one but was then disarmed with the rest. The next that Machiavelli saw of Cesare was as the Duke was riding through the town to suppress the rioting that had commenced. Seeing Machiavelli, he called out: 'You see, I know how to make use of opportunity. Tell your masters that I have done a great service for them.' Writing on that same night of 31 December Machiavelli told the Signoria: 'The city is still being sacked. I am in the greatest difficulties—it may not be possible to find a messenger to deliver this letter. Tomorrow I shall send more news. However, I think it unlikely that they [the *condottieri*] will be alive by the morning.'

Paolo and Francesco Orsini survived that night—their powerful kinsman the Cardinal was in Rome and Cesare was uncertain of the reactions if the Orsini were executed immediately. But Vitellozzo and Oliverotto were strangled, seated back to back. They died badly, Oliverotto crying for mercy and attempting to throw the blame on Vitellozzo, Vitellozzo beseeching the Duke to persuade his father to grant him indulgence for his sins.

In Rome, Alexander adopted a simplified form of the same stratagem to lay hands on Cardinal Orsini. The Cardinal was invited to the Vatican Palace where he was arrested and taken to Sant' Angelo where he died—probably from poison. His possessions were confiscated, his household turned into the street. His mother, who had lived with him 'was driven out of her home with her serving maids: no one would give them shelter for all were afraid and they wandered through the streets of Rome'. The Orsini in Cesare's hands were deprived of what little protection they had enjoyed and they were strangled as soon as Cesare knew that it was safe to do so.

'The dragon that devours lesser serpents': such was the opinion of those not immediately involved in the events in Romagna. The deadly swiftness and efficiency with which a group of dangerous men had been eliminated as though they were inexperienced boys completed the legend of Cesare's invincibility. The Vitelli family abandoned their state of Città di Castello, the Baglione fled from Perugia. Cesare's march south from the Romagna to Rome was less a military campaign than a hunting expedition with frightened men running for cover as soon as the now formidable army appeared. City after city fell, or hastened to accept him, so that within a month of the *coup d'état* at Sinigaglia, the greater part of the Papal States was under his firm control. There was a brief rebellion of the few surviving barons in the south, hereditary enemies combining in sheer desperation to save what they could. They achieved little enough, saving their lives but not their possessions.

Cesare came to Rome to confer with his father. There seems to have been a difference of opinion between the two, Alexander expressing anxiety at the sudden, tumultuous speed of Cesare's success. But there was no clash between father and son. Again, Rome was under the son's dominance. There was now an element of the mysterious in Cesare's habits. Rarely was he seen in daylight, and then he was usually masked. 'He is known to be in Rome, but very few people see him,' the Venetian ambassador reported. 'The Pope does not refer to him—and so I shall pretend ignorance unless he mentions it. The Duke's actions are incomprehensible to everyone.' Cesare had always delighted in disguises and mysterious movements, employing them to enhance that element of unpredictability which was a valuable political weapon. But his masked, nocturnal prowlings in Rome during the spring of 1503 probably sprang from a personal motive. It was widely believed that the disease he had contracted had rendered his face repulsive, a bitter experience for a once handsome man and one that could explain the savagery that attended his actions in Rome.

In that summer, Cesare was at the zenith of his career. Louis of France was now more colleague than master, for the French had been heavily defeated in Naples and Louis needed Cesare more than Cesare needed him. The Papal States were virtually his personal possession; the neighbouring states were either allied or afraid so that his influence was strong throughout central Italy. Alexander even considered erecting a monarchy on the foundation of the Papal States, so that his son could be styled King. That plan foundered on French opposition, but there was another and, in the long term, even better plan—the passing of the tiara to Cesare. Alexander made the suggestion explicit when wooing the Venetians. 'After my death either he, or you, shall have the crown.' There was no reason why Cesare should not pick up his discarded cardinal's hat as preliminary to assuming the papal tiara.

All things seemed possible in August 1503. Alexander was in the best of health and could look forward to a span of life long enough to allow Cesare to exploit the existing situation under the protection of the Papacy. The great dreams ended, abruptly, on 12 August when both Cesare and his father fell dangerously ill. The illness proved mortal for Alexander, who died on the 18th: Cesare survived, but was still confined to his sick-room during the confused and dangerous period that inevitably followed the death of a pope.

7. Flight and Death

The Sant'Angelo bridge and the Angel's Tower, Rome (J. Allan Cash)

'He told me himself that he had foreseen every obstacle that could arise on the death of his father, and had prepared adequate remedies. But he could not foresee that, at the time of his father's death, his own life would be in such imminent hazard.'

Machiavelli was again with Cesare, sent to Rome by his government to keep close watch on the rapidly changing situation. He was able to confirm that the rumours of poison were merely rumours: both father and son had been struck down by the deadly fever that haunted the Campagna in high summer. Cesare was still extremely weak, but remained sufficiently alert to order Michelotto to raid the papal treasury. While Alexander's dishonoured corpse was still awaiting burial, Michelotto forced an entry into the Vatican with a strong escort and got away with 100,000 ducats as well as a quantity of silverware.

But that was the last effective action Cesare was able to execute.

While he was on his sick-bed, the complex intrigues which preceded a new Conclave were under way. They resulted in a stop-gap election, the octogenarian Cardinal of Siena emerging as Pope Pius III. He at least was neutral towards Cesare, but what hopes the sick man might have cherished were extinguished three weeks later when Pius died, his senile condition not proving equal to the rigorous demands made upon it. And again the complex machinery of the Conclave was set in motion—but on this occasion the prime favourite was Cardinal Giuliano della Rovere, the acknowledged enemy of the house of Borgia.

Even before it was known that della Rovere's chances were high, Cesare's position was desperate. His army had vanished overnight, the Spaniards marching to join the Spanish forces in the south, the French recalled by Louis for his own purposes. Cesare's innumerable enemies had taken swift advantage of his weakness and, throughout the States of the Church, the dispossessed lords had returned and had the common sense to make an alliance for mutual self-protection. In Rome itself, the Orsini were seeking vengeance on the now helpless invalid and it was only because he had managed to secure the impregnable fortress of Sant' Angelo that Cesare continued to survive.

But he still had one strong card to play in the coming papal election—a very high proportion of the Sacred College consisted of Spaniards or other creatures of the Borgia regime. He could still directly influence the election. And he chose to instruct his supporters to vote for—Cardinal Giuliano della Rovere.

In Machiavelli's opinion it was his biggest mistake, and proved fatal for him. The man he should have supported was the Frenchman, Georges d'Amboise. Cesare judged, perhaps, that della Rovere was almost certain to emerge successful even without the Spanish votes and when della Rovere approached him, with the promise of confirming him in the Dukedom of Romagna in return for his support, he decided to bet upon the certainty. Machiavelli put his finger on the obvious weakness in the arrangement. 'It is difficult to see how the Pope can be forced to keep his promise. Everyone knows how great is the hatred he holds for Borgia. The Duke is acting blindly. He seems to believe that other people, at least, will keep their word.'

On 1 November 1503 della Rovere was elected pope and, almost as though mocking Cesare, took the name of Julius II. He was playing with Cesare exactly as Cesare had played with so many men. He wanted the return of the Romagna to its rightful lord—the pope—

Julius II, by Raphael (Mansell Collection)

before the Venetians moved into the temporary vacuum of power. Some of the cities—notably Cesena and Forli—were still faithful to Cesare and small garrisons of his men were dotted throughout his erstwhile dukedom. Julius had not the smallest aversion to fighting when it was necessary, but it seemed to him possible to take over Cesare's territories with the minimum of expenditure. It was for this reason that, even now, he pretended to be considering the confirmation of Cesare both as Gonfaloniere and Duke. He even corresponded with Florence to arrange a safe-conduct, and allowed Cesare to leave Rome.

But Cesare had got only as far as Ostia when Pope Julius struck. He demanded that Cesare should yield up the passwords of the fortresses of Forli and Cesena. Cesare refused. He was promptly arrested and brought back to Rome and, at the same time, the last remnant of his military power was shattered. His bodyguard, under the command of Michelotto, was destroyed and Michelotto himself carried off to stand trial for 'the deaths of many people, including the Duke of Gandia, the Lord of Camerino and his sons, the Lord of Faenza, Duke Alfonso of Bisceglie. . . .'

Cesare's arrest was the effective end of his power. The influential Venetian ambassador showed the decisive change in public opinion when he refused to call upon Cesare, although Cesare had urgently requested him. Gradually, word spread through Rome that his once iron will was now broken, that Cesare, the man who had once looked upon either triumph or disaster with the same apparent indifference was now a weeping wreck, full of self-pity and apologies. There was report of a poignant interview between him and one of his late victims, Guidobaldo Montefeltre, when Cesare fell on his knees, grovelling, begging for pardon, promising to return the art treasures he had stolen from Urbino. Julius, whether by accident or design, had confined him in the very room in the Vatican where Lucrezia's husband Alfonso had been murdered. Cesare, it was stated, wept and protested. It was probable that his total collapse was attributable to his illness but, in the cold eyes of Renaissance diplomats, the effect was the same. It was now that Machiavelli revised his opinion of the man he had once thought might be leader of a united Italy. In his eyes there had been two Cesares. The splendid Duke Valentino would survive, enshrined for all time as The Prince, but the cowering, chattering invalid was fit only for a gallery of second-rate failures.

On 29 January Cesare was again a free man—but a man stripped of even the appearances of power: in return for his freedom he signed over all his rights in the Romagna. He was still Duke of Valenti-

nois, but Louis was cooling as rapidly as the rest of Cesare's quondam allies and it was as little more than a mercenary that Cesare
turned south to Naples. There, his Spanish kinsmen were preparing
a massive drive to the north which would throw the French out of
Italy and it was natural that the Great Captain, Gonsalvo, should
take such a *condottiero* as Cesare Borgia into Spanish pay. He had now
totally recovered from his illness and seemed again his old, supremely confident self as he prepared for a campaign that, as a by product,
would probably reinstate him in the Romagna.

Then, on the night of 26 May, his commander and comrade-in-
arms Gonsalvo, arrested him on direct orders from Spain. Julius
had made it very clear to King Ferdinand of Spain that he would take
it grievously amiss if Cesare were even indirectly aided, and Ferdinand, seeing no reason to put himself out for a discredited

77

Ferdinand of Spain (Mansell Collection)

78

condottiero, closed Cesare's career in Italy with as neat an act of treachery as any Cesare had himself executed. From Naples he was shipped to Spain. Rumour had it that the widow of the first Duke of Gandia was demanding vengeance on her husband's murderer but Ferdinand probably felt that Cesare might still have some value as counter for bargaining. He was treated well enough at first and was even able to correspond with his sister. Lucrezia did all that she could to secure his release but no one saw any profit to be made out of it, and he remained imprisoned until he succeeded in escaping two years after his arrest.

There was only one place left that might give him refuge, and that was the kingdom of his brother-in-law, Jean d'Albret, King of Navarre. France had turned him down, Louis replying to his request for asylum with the information that not only was he unwelcome but that he had been deprived of his Dukedom of Valentinois on the grounds that he had joined the Spanish enemies of France. Cesare therefore turned to the family he had virtually forgotten. In the Easter of 1502 there had been plans to bring his wife Charlotte to Italy, but they had been frustrated, Louis proving reluctant to part with a useful hostage. Charlotte's brother had good cause to welcome Cesare now—as mercenary soldier, not as prince. The tiny kingdom of Navarre, caught up between its giant neighbours, was itself split between two warring factions. Cesare's task was to suppress his brother-in-law's enemies at home and afterwards, perhaps, defend Navarre from the encroachments of France and Spain. There was talk of supplying him later with men to begin his conquests anew—but events proved otherwise.

In March 1507 Cesare was employed at a task in which he was supremely expert—the siege of a citadel. The castle of Viana was held by the rebel vassal of the King, and had been holding out with considerable success for some months. Cesare invested it with a large force and sat down to the tedious business of battering a fortress into submission. On the morning of the 12th a minor skirmish broke out some distance from the main body—a skirmish which was probably designed as an ambush. Cesare galloped forward at the head of thirty men, and was immediately cut off as a body emerged from the castle. His horse was killed in the first moments but he continued fighting on foot with great courage 'nevertheless he was killed, and his body cut into nine pieces. So died Valentino, richly deserving death for all the evils he had wrought in Italy.'

'He merited the most miserable death,' Machiavelli concurred.

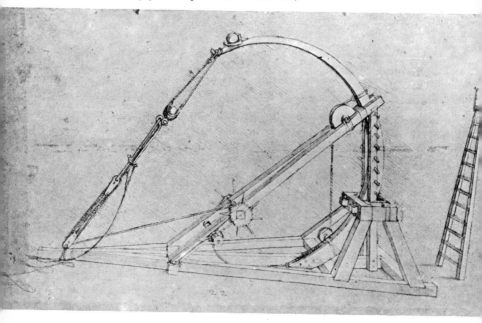

'He was a man devoid of pity, a rebel against Christ, a poison-breathing hydra.' It was reasonable that the foremost political theorist of Italy should so dismiss his quondam hero for Cesare Borgia—Duke of Valentinois, Duke of Romagna, Prince of Andria, Gonfaloniere of Holy Church—committed the only real crime known to Renaissance diplomacy. He failed.

Cesare's wife Charlotte—the derelict duchess of French romance—retired to a convent and survived her husband by seven years, dying while still a young woman. Their daughter Louise was twice married, the second time into the Bourbon family, but made no particular mark of her own. Two other, natural, children of Cesare's were brought up in Ferrara, presumably under his sister's protection. The girl became an abbess, the boy disappeared—to turn up nearly fifty years later in Paris asking the King for aid on the ground that his father had served France well. They gave him 100 ducats and sent him home.

In Italy, the Borgia family survived the storm that had destroyed Cesare but now, without his dynamism, it sank into respectable obscurity. His younger brother Joffre settled safely in Naples with his Neapolitan wife Sancia. Ironically, the flighty Sancia who had caused such trouble in Rome proved to be barren and it was through a second wife that Joffre obtained the heirs to his modest estate.

Their mother Vanozza passed her remaining years between fighting for her property in law courts and amassing heavenly credit through the medium of pious works. She became something of a tourist attraction in Rome, but conducted herself with immense respectability and, in her will, she left her considerable property to the Church.

Giulia Farnese not only survived the loss of her protector Alexander but even managed to marry her daughter by him to the nephew of his great enemy, Pope Julius. In this matter, at least, Julius was an apt pupil of Machiavelli's, judging an action solely on the grounds of its expediency.

Lucrezia made perhaps the greatest personal change of them all, proving beyond a doubt that she had been the passive tool of her father and brother. In due course she became Duchess of Ferrara and presided over a court of considerable culture, earning high praise both for her intellectual abilities and her moral life. Her son by her beloved second husband, Alfonso of Bisceglie, died, to her immense grief. But her children by Este survived to ascend the ducal throne so that it was solely in Ferrara, and under another name, that some of Alexander's dynastic hopes were fulfilled.

Lucrezia died, before her fortieth year, in 1519. In her last years she had turned to religion, not with the ostentation of her mother, but with a deep and quiet conviction nowhere better expressed than in the letter she wrote to the Pope a few hours before her death. She knew that she was dying and begged his high blessing on her passing. 'I approach the end of my life with pleasure knowing that in a few hours, after receiving for the last time all the holy Sacraments of the Church, I shall find release.'

Cesare Borgia, by Giorgione (Radio Times Hulton Picture Library)

Summary of Events

1453: *Fall of Constantinople*
1455: Calixtus III (Borgia), Pope
1456: Rodrigo Borgia, Cardinal
1458?: Pedro, 1st Duke of Gandia, born
1461: *Edward IV, King of England*
1469: *Marriage of Ferdinand and Isabella*
1474: Juan Borgia, son of Rodrigo by Vanozza, born
1475: Cesare Borgia, son of Rodrigo by Vanozza, born
1480: Lucrezia Borgia, daughter of Rodrigo by Vanozza, born
1482: Joffre Borgia, son of Rodrigo by Vanozza, born
1483: *Charles VIII, King of France*
Richard III, King of England
1485: *Henry VII, King of England*
1488: Death of Pedro, 1st Duke of Gandia
Juan Borgia, 2nd Duke of Gandia
1492: Alexander VI (Borgia), Pope
Columbus discovers America
1493: Cesare Borgia, Cardinal
First marriage of Lucrezia (to Giovanni Sforza)
1494: Charles VIII invades Italy
1497: Murder of Juan, 2nd Duke of Gandia
1498: Second marriage of Lucrezia (to Alfonso of Bisceglie)
Cesare Borgia relinquishes cardinalate
Louis XII, King of France
1499: Cesare Borgia, Duke of Valentinois
Louis XII invades Italy
1500: Cesare Borgia, Duke of Romagna
Murder of Alfonso of Bisceglie
1501: Third marriage of Lucrezia (to Alfonso of Ferrara)
1503: Death of Alexander VI
Pius III Pope
Julius II Pope
1504–6: Cesare Borgia in captivity
1507: Death of Cesare Borgia
1509: *Henry VIII, King of England*
1513: Death of Julius II
1519: Death of Lucrezia Borgia.

A Select Bibliography

Auton, Jean d'. *Chroniques de Louis XII*. 1889

Breisach, Ernst. *Caterina Sforza*. 1968

Burchard, John (ed. L. Thuasne). *Diarium*. 1885. Selections relative to the reign of Alexander VI have been translated and edited by Geoffrey Parker under the title of *At the Court of the Borgia*. 1963

Burckhardt, Jacob. *The Civilisation of the Renaissance in Italy*. Translated S. G. C. Middlemore, 1921.

Conti, Sigismondo de'. *Le storie de suoi tempi (1475–1510)*. 1883

Giustiniani, Antonio (ed. Pasquale Villari). *Dispacci 1502–5*. 1876

Gregorovius, Ferdinand. *History of the City of Rome in the Middle Ages*: Vol. VII, pts I and II. Translated Annie Hamilton. 1900

Gregorovius, Ferdinand. *Lucretia Borgia: according to original documents and correspondence of her day*. Translated John Leslie Gardner. 1903

Machiavelli, Niccolo. *The Prince: Murder of Vitellozzo etc.* Bohn's Library. 1847

Pastor, Ludwig. *The History of the Popes*: Vols V and VI. 1898

Pulver, Jeffrey *Machiavelli*. 1937

Rolfe, Frederick ('Baron Corvo'). *Chronicles of the House of Borgia*. 1901

Sanuto, Marino. *Diarii*: Vols I–V. 1879

Symonds, J. A. *Renaissance in Italy. Age of the Despots*. 1897

Yriarte, Charles. *La Vie de Cesare Borgia*. 1889